EMPLOYEE MORALE

EMPLOYEE MORALE

Driving Performance in Challenging Times

David Bowles

Managing Director, Research & Consulting International,
Rancho Santa Fe, California

and

Cary Cooper

Pro Vice Chancellor (External Relations)
and
Professor of Organizational Psychology
and Health, Lancaster University

palgrave
macmillan

First published 2009 by
PALGRAVE MACMILLAN

Palgrave Macmillan in the UK is an imprint of Macmillan Publishers Limited,
registered in England, company number 785998, of Houndmills, Basingstoke,
Hampshire RG21 6XS.

Palgrave Macmillan in the US is a division of St Martin's Press LLC,
175 Fifth Avenue, New York, NY 10010.

Palgrave Macmillan is the global academic imprint of the above companies
and has companies and representatives throughout the world.

Palgrave® and Macmillan® are registered trademarks in the United States,
the United Kingdom, Europe and other countries

ISBN-13: 978–0–230–57942–2

This book is printed on paper suitable for recycling and made from fully
managed and sustained forest sources. Logging, pulping and manufacturing
processes are expected to conform to the environmental regulations of the
country of origin.

A catalogue record for this book is available from the British Library.

A catalog record for this book is available from the Library of Congress.

10 9 8 7 6 5 4 3 2 1
18 17 16 15 14 13 12 11 10 09

Printed and bound in Great Britain by
CPI Antony Rowe, Chippenham and Eastbourne

CONTENTS

CONTENTS

LIST OF FIGURES, TABLES AND CHARTS

Figures

Tables

Charts

ACKNOWLEDGMENTS

DAVID BOWLES

My first acknowledgment and dedication belongs to my beloved Janice, without whom this book would not have been possible; I also dedicate the book to my wonderful mother, sisters and extended family in England; to my friends at Starbucks Del Mar Heights who cajoled, encouraged, criticized and contributed ideas to make the book better. Many thanks go out to the employees at Starbucks Torrey Hills, who kept me in coffee and support while most of the book was written, and to authors before me who demonstrated convincingly that large parts of a book could indeed be written in a Café! One of those Starbucks employees, Ryan Shue, deserves special thanks for sitting down for a long interview on military morale and his experiences in that area as a US Marine. Professor Mika Kivimäki of UCL, London, was a great help in understanding some of the issues related to her extensive and thorough research on morale and employee health. Thanks too for the use of the University of California, San Diego, Geisel library facilities, open almost around the clock and so comfortable and comprehensive, which allowed me to research this book and write large sections of it.

Our support at Palgrave Macmillan has been 110 percent and I am especially grateful to Stephen Rutt for agreeing almost instantly to our proposal for a book linking morale and performance, to Eleanor Davey-Corrigan for making it all run so smoothly, and to Macmillan Publishing Solutions in Bangalore for their speedy and excellent copy editing.

Several companies have contributed their help and shared part of their intellectual property with us in order to bring you the best morale research that there is. Many thanks go out to Hilti Group in Liechtenstein, and its Chairman, Dr Pius Baschera, for agreeing to share their data and be our Case Study. Hilti lives what we talk about in this book. Thanks also to Klaus Risch, current Executive VP and Global head of HR at Hilti; also to Andre Siegenthaler, formerly in that job at Hilti, who was such a great client and friend while the Hilti data were being collected a few years back.

We both very much appreciate the following organizations for giving us access to their data:

The Gallup Organization; Mercer; Accenture; Sirota Survey Intelligence; American Society for Quality; American Marketing Association; Rowman & Littlefield Publishing Group; American Psychological Association; MIT-Sloan Management Review; Taylor and Francis (Productivity Press); BAI Banking Intelligence.

Finally, I would like to make a special dedication to two dear friends: my former consulting partner Dr Marshall Whitmire, who worked tirelessly to see that our small research and consulting firm kept clients happy around the world; and my friend and colleague of almost 40 years, Cary Cooper, who has taught, inspired, encouraged and believed in me for all that time. It is an honor to write a book with him.

CARY COOPER

I learned a great deal about morale and camaraderie from all my former Ph.D. students, who supported and valued me throughout my career – this book is dedicated to them.

INTRODUCTION

Being in the morale business, we experience something like doctors who go to cocktail parties and accidentally let the fact of their profession slip out, resulting in all sorts of symptoms being "shared", and diagnoses requested. Mention "work morale" to a perfect stranger and they respond with a knowing laugh, a groan and always, always the same comment: "You should come to *my* work place!!" Are they asking us to come because things are so great? Not judging by the comments which follow their invitation, no. Details of the "boss from hell", the "colleague from hell" or the "company from hell" follow. Of course, when asked how long they have been there, and hearing "fifteen years", the question begs to be asked "then why stay so long?" The answer is usually quick, sure-footed, something like "I love the people there" (except for the boss or colleague from hell, of course), "I love the job", "great benefits" and so on. This is the essence of the complex of human emotions and related opinions we call "morale", the mix of positive and negative, this feeling we have at and about our work, where we spend so much of our waking time. As much as we complain, too, let's remember that when a person takes him or herself out of the workforce through retirement or other reasons, the result is often painful for that individual, sometimes even fatal. Is it just a coincidence that, even after a day's work in environments of varying sustenance, as far as morale is concerned, many of us sit down to watch *The Office* on TV or read Dilbert cartoons*? Work has such a hold on us, and for more reasons than the money, as we shall see. Clearly, how we feel at and about work, our morale, plays an important part in our *broader ongoing life*.

The Office, which originated in the UK, features a format which often covered morale issues; it was brought over to the United States where it has enjoyed significant success; Dilbert cartoons feature a character who works in an office cubicle and makes fun of the many absurdities of work life.

In the past, these typical complaints and negative reactions about work which people gave us when we met them might not have been seen as so important, just accepted as "the way things are" and laughed off; but now that we know so much more about the connection between *morale and organization performance* (internally on factors such as productivity and financial performance, externally on measures of customer satisfaction and so on), *they have taken on far greater significance*. Now raised from just "touchy-feely" to "mission critical", employee morale is finally getting the attention which it deserves. As it does, organizations are changing everything from their structure to their processes to take account of this fact, and starting to manage themselves around the need to measure and improve morale on an ongoing basis. Starting with the hiring process, to every single promotion and via ongoing methods which we will detail, morale is more and more the focus and high morale the goal. Of course, not all do this, but we can safely say from many years of direct observation and work around the world that the best, most successful, most creative and dynamic organizations use various social-scientific and management methods to continually or frequently *measure, provide feedback and take action to achieve the highest possible state of morale among their workforce.*

Our goal with this book is to explore these issues in depth for you, to provide you with an understanding of morale, why it is so important, how it is measured in the best organizations, and how its power can be tapped to create extraordinary gains in productivity, customer loyalty, and (if you have such things) financial results. If you are new to this field, we hope to give you a sense of the anticipation and excitement which even very experienced senior management teams (who have seen everything) feel when they receive the results of their yearly employee opinion surveys; these results spell out exactly how morale is holding up around their organizational areas of responsibility (large or small). This interest level is hardly limited to the top ranks; employees at all levels in so many surveys have told us that, in terms of organizational communications, *"the results of this survey"* have their attention above and beyond anything else. If you have experience in the field, we hope to take this to a deeper level, making connections which you might not have known existed.

High morale creates all these positive effects by giving all levels of employee a sense of psychological "well-being", which is the driving force for such gains. But make no mistake: this is far distant from a quick fix of "casual Fridays" clothing to create a warm and fuzzy feeling for a while. Taking the road toward high morale is a long-term investment by an organization, a comprehensive task not undertaken by the timid, those who would rather live by the "image" of change than real change, those who wish to hold onto control at any cost, and those who do not wish to change their *own* thinking and behavior (maybe even beliefs and habits they have held on to for many years), because it requires all these things.

Our title contains a phrase which we would like to explain: "Driving Performance" is our core thesis and refers to a fundamental *causal connection* between employee morale and how well your organization can function, which we will explain and demonstrate with a wide range of research, a case study and other anecdotal evidence. In order to help you achieve a high level of morale so that you can benefit from its many performance advantages, three stages of action are necessary and they will be covered extensively in this book:

- The first stage of morale-driven performance improvement comes from investing in processes which lead to measuring morale in a scientifically valid way. There are many ways to collect this data and many pitfalls along the way. We want you to know the best practices to bring you to the point of having excellent data, in which you can have confidence as a basis for further action. Without this foundation, one builds on shaky ground indeed.
- The second stage involves correctly interpreting the data you receive, and from having the ability to dig deeply into that data to find the real gems which can change the way you see your organization and perhaps even the way you do business.
- The third stage happens once you have this data, have looked into in with the best tools, and begin to implement change. Morale encompasses so much that it can be difficult to know where to turn, and especially what to do at first. What have other organizations done here? What works and what does not? Does this depend on the type of organization you are, the business you are in? Or does "one size fit all"? We plan to answer these questions for you.

We will use various sources of data to back up our statements in this book, so let us briefly share those. Our first source will be personal experience: we are a transatlantic writing team, having been born, raised and educated on opposite sides of that ocean. We then swapped countries, and apart from 6 years of working together in the United Kingdom in the 70s, have lived in each other's native country ever since.

We mention this because our plan is to bring you an international perspective on morale. It is one of those areas which certainly is affected by culture, and the experience of having both lived and worked in the United States, the United Kingdom and many other countries is important. (To counter questions which arise in the literature about the "Anglo-US" focus of much work on organization culture, morale, etc. we will give examples from several cultures from outside that particular geographic axis.) We estimate that we have more than 60 man-years of teaching and consulting experience between the two of us, focused on people issues in organizations. This includes working for consulting firms (including ones we have ourselves founded) which have surveyed well over a million people at work; personally interviewing more than a thousand executives from all major industrial, non-profit and governmental sectors in one-on-one sessions, focused on strategic human resource issues; running hundreds of morale-based focus groups with thousands of employees at all levels in organizations throughout the United States and Europe, as well as in Asia; analyzing the data from many, many employee surveys, and conducting hundreds of feedback sessions on morale for some of the world's largest organizations down to small rural hospitals. This has allowed us to see what works, and what does not; what "best practices" are out there; and what mistakes can be made (and there are many).

For the second source, we will update you with recent data from consultants who are collecting it on a daily basis, to show you important trends in employee morale, worldwide; some of this is proprietary, and some in the public domain. Data, of course, is only as good as the process by which it is collected and analyzed. We will show you how best to collect and look at this type of information, what questions can be answered by it, and what simple statistical techniques can tap its power (and yet are neglected by so many organizations generating this data). We present a case study of an organization which has successfully managed their morale profile to a stellar level, *and has remained that way*; and we will finally draw conclusions from what has been discussed and show you how to take advantage of this knowledge to maximize your returns on the entire morale-improvement process.

Our approach, then, is both anecdotal and data-driven. We find that this is a mix which works in a field like this, based as it is on human behavior and emotions.

No longer relegated to the "less serious" aspects of management (the "serious" being of course finance and strategy), organization morale has come of age. Our wish is that by the time you finish reading, you, too, will have become a morale "fan", enthused and empowered to help make high morale a reality where you work.

David Bowles
San Diego, California, USA
Cary L Cooper
Lancaster, UK
July 2009

CHAPTER 1

WHAT IS MORALE?

Early on in our consulting practice, at the end of an employee survey, managers representing different parts of the organization would be presented with the results, a process which often took a couple of hours and involved looking at massive amounts of data, question by question, group by group. At the end they would frequently ask an important question about their own area: "I saw the presentation, but can you tell me how my group did?" As easy as the task of answering this may sound, it is not: how do you "boil down" the results of 110 questions into one quick summary? They had seen the results on the screen, even summarized by major topics like "compensation and benefits", "communications", etc., but they often had no real sense of the overall picture. At the time, the tactic which was used was to say something like this:

> Well, your employees love their jobs but don't feel so good about the company; they think many more decisions should be made at the local level and that they are being micro-managed by corporate. As you saw, your group was lower than the company average on a few questions, but also higher on others.

To which they would reply, quiet appropriately:

> Yes, I noticed that, but how did we *do*?

They were asking about *morale*; they wanted the big picture, the sense as to whether people in their group were feeling good or bad about *things in general*. That was a long time ago; nowadays, as we shall see, sophisticated software is used to "slice and dice" the data to create everything from overall morale-index scores to subindices such as "engagement". Go to a good external consultant now, or use skilled in-house resources, and those questions are easily answered.

Most people have a sense of what morale is; we have heard the word in many contexts, for example in the military, and often where we work. The dictionary is quite clear on the subject, so let's start there:

Morale:

1. a state of individual psychological well-being based upon a sense of confidence and usefulness and purpose.
2. the spirit of a group that makes the members want the group to succeed [syn: esprit de corps].[1]

Other sources add things such as:

"willingness to perform assigned tasks"[2]

The phrase "psychological well-being" appears in this definition, something which is very familiar to readers in Europe (but much less so in the United States, where "well-being" is generally used to refer to physical states rather than psychological). We also see that morale refers to an individual as well as a group, it is about confidence and a sense of purpose at the individual level (we would argue at the group level too) as well as the "spirit" of a group. Psychological states are referenced, motivation is covered too, morale is said to create a "willingness to perform assigned tasks". In other words, this little word carries a lot of weight.

Note that morale is defined in a way that goes far beyond just "feeling good". The latter may be a by-product of high morale but does "feeling good" by itself make people "want the group to succeed"? Not necessarily. It could make you want to take the day off and go to the beach. In other words, morale is a psychological state which makes a person want to contribute, be a part of things, make things work better, more successfully.

The measurement of morale has been around a long time, starting in earnest in the postwar United States, around 1947. That means plenty of time has passed for the meaning of this word to be transformed, for it to be used in many different settings, for new ideas and words to emerge which challenge its usefulness or create more focus on a particular aspect. So perhaps it's not surprising that people get confused when looking at all the words which have come to be used in this field.

Consider the following phrases:

Employee* Morale
Employee Satisfaction
Employee Well-Being
Employee Engagement
Employee Commitment
Employee Involvement
Employee Passion
Employee Empowerment
Employee Enthusiasm

Do they refer, in some way, to the same thing? Or are they quite different? The answer is that some do indeed mean the same thing as morale, while others (like "engagement") do not, and yet are sometimes used as if they do. It is important to find our way around this word maze so that we can deepen our understanding of morale. One important issue here: *we will use definitions which are used in the non-academic business and organizational world rather than the academic one*. These can be quite different, with the latter requiring much greater adherence to specific words. Our experience is that consulting professionals and their clients in the community of organizations for whom they work do not care nearly as much about a high level of precision in using exactly one word or another, and use them in far less precise but practical ways that might make some members of the academic community's hair stand on end.

Employee Satisfaction is a good example of this. In the everyday life of a consultant with her clients, or a typical Corporate CEO, it is often just another proxy for morale. Strictly speaking though, it refers to those areas of work life where employees can be satisfied or dissatisfied, such as with their pay, the amount of information they receive, their organization in general or the lighting in their work area. When those opinions are aggregated, there is an overall level of satisfaction. Of course, not all work life aspects are things about which we are *satisfied* or not; sometimes we measure whether employees *understand*

---

* We chose to use the word "employee" throughout this book, mindful of the fact that a significant number of organizations prefer "associate", "partner", "team member" or other words to describe their relationship with the work force.

something, not whether they are satisfied with it. Other aspects of work morale that are measured might include whether something is present or not (a clear sense of direction, for example). Is this satisfaction? Strictly speaking it is not, unless we have a follow-on question to the one which asks if something is present, which asks the person *how they feel about it*. For most intents and purposes, though, outside the halls of academia, satisfaction is not limited in this way and is used like the word morale.

Well-Being, when used to talk about the emotional state of employees at work as opposed to their physical health, is easier to define and is mostly used in Europe as a proxy for morale.

Engagement is currently the most widely used word in our field. It is certainly cresting in popularity, and that wave may last a while. This is an interesting phenomenon for some of us who have been in the morale business a long time: on the one hand it is exciting to see people so enthusiastic about morale, no matter what they call it. Having said that, it is not really so new a concept. Just like in the medical profession or clinical psychology, where diagnoses come into "fashion" for a while, before fading away and being replaced by the "next big thing", there is similar activity in this field. Words and concepts which have been used for decades lose popularity and are replaced by new ones, and books are written, explaining to us that an organization cannot possibly succeed without this or that. Such is the case with "engagement". But is this new wine or is it old wine in new bottles? And what exactly is engagement?

Engagement is generally seen by its biggest enthusiasts as a *higher level emotional state, beyond simply an elevated level of morale*, in which employees feel a strong bond with their organization and will go the extra mile for it. For example, they willingly volunteer for work, even outside their area, if it helps the organization. They are not the ones who rush out at 5 p.m. sharp, regardless of what needs to be done and how important it is for a customer. Their level of resistance is low, in a positive sense (they don't say "no" to everything that is asked of them). If this sounds a lot like a high morale individual as we (and the dictionary) have defined it, that is true! The one area where one can argue that engagement might reach past high morale is the crucial element called *advocacy*. This means that an engaged employee is more likely to be an advocate for the organization, such as in recommending it to friends as a place to work or to potential customers as a trusted supplier of goods or services. Fans of morale might also argue, though, that high morale employees also show strong signs of advocacy. For these reasons, engagement and high morale have such common ground that they are often used interchangeably.

For the engagement purist though, one can have relatively good *overall morale* and yet not such a large percentage of truly "engaged" employees, because by their definition they are the *crème de la crème* of high morale workers. This is why the international consultancy and opinion pollster Gallup indicates that *only 29 percent of US employees are engaged at work*, a shocking number given the positive benefits which flow from such a state.[3]

If we are to attempt a fusion of morale and engagement, it is this: *engagement is a by-product of high morale, a result of it*. When workplace psychosocial and physical environmental factors are perceived positively by the workforce, they experience a sense of well-being which we call high morale. When that morale level is high enough, it triggers behaviors on the part of workers which include the ones we have described above (advocacy, willingness to "go the extra mile", commitment, helping others, etc.) and which we call "engagement". Engagement is therefore not possible without high morale; and high morale usually results in engagement.

Employee Enthusiasm, Passion and Commitment are all used to describe various levels of emotional attachment to, and feeling for, the job and the organization. They are all to be found in highly engaged workforces and those with high overall morale.

Employee Involvement describes the extent to which management creates a work situation which is less "top down" and more collaborative; an example of this would be soliciting input such as ideas on to how to make things better at work, thus giving a greater degree of creativity and a "voice" to workers.

With *employee empowerment*, there is an extension of involvement, in that both involve some devolution of power to the individual worker; however, empowerment goes further through delegation of decision-making authority, often through the use of a flatter organization structure, for example. Self-directed work teams are an example of employee empowerment.

If we keep in mind one important thing about morale at work, which is that it is a *general psychological state of well-being*, we can begin to construct a model of what influences this state. In order to do that, we will first take a very short walk through the history of how workers have been seen in the past and how far we have come in that perception. Following this we will examine the elements in the workplace which affect how we feel there.

WORK LIFE OVER THE AGES

It's fair to say that for much of "work"* history the view of Mankind has been of a rather primitive species, requiring various forms of coercion to do almost anything beyond take basic care of itself. This "beast"-like view still lives on in some office and factory settings, and is epitomized in the message on the T-shirt which one of us created as an annual client gift (it was an all-time "most popular item", which must say something):

The Beatings Will Continue Until Morale Improves

While we do not make him the source of the viewpoint on this T-shirt in any way, a man by the name of Frederick Taylor (1856–1915)[4] institutionalized this general view of the nature of Man with his writings, focusing very much on the need for "control" and "enforcement" at work in order to create a more productive and efficient work environment. The famous Ford production lines were a result of this philosophy. Taylor's view did not leave much room for the intelligence of the average worker, in fact for anything inside the person at all. His "scientific management" was focused on the processes for managing the workflow, not on any science of human behavior. In spite of this somewhat negative capsule description of his work, Taylor's legacy did lead to huge increases in productivity of workers and an equally impressive increase in their standard of living.

His view lasted until a more "enlightened age" began to come about. We see this happening after World War II, which period coincided with the emergence of methodologies to study and measure morale. It was certainly moved forward by the seminal contribution of

---

* By "work" we mean that period when Man started to become an "employee" with a "boss", perhaps not by name but by function. The caveman "worked", but not in the sense we mean here.

Douglas M. McGregor (1906–64)[5] who took the work of Taylor and that of Elton Mayo, the founder of the human relations movement, and positioned them as *Theory X and Theory Y*.

The enlightened view (Theory Y) brought forward the novel idea that humans actually wanted to work, that it had some intrinsic value to us even beyond the financial and that we had a lot to contribute which need not be beaten, enforced or controlled out of us. Indeed, as this viewpoint was extended, the idea was put forward that all that was necessary was to *lessen the obstacles to the emergence of motivation, creativity, innovation and the desire to contribute*; often these obstacles were seen in the ranks of management. Interestingly, therefore, the evolution of thought went from a place where coercive management was indispensable to efficient workplace functioning, to the point lately where management is often seen as *the very obstacle which prevents this from happening*!

Our position is that we subscribe to the latter idea up to a point, that is, less management is better than more; that it can and does get in the way of efficiency and even high morale. But we don't go all the way to advocate complete elimination of this function, because there is still the question of leadership: who will set the tone, drive the culture, inspire and have the intellectual power to forge ahead strategically? If this sounds like TOP management, that is correct: we are more sanguine about the role of middle management, and will discuss this later in greater detail.

BUILDING A MODEL OF ORGANIZATIONAL MORALE

The base on which we will build our model of morale is as follows:

Almost everything which happens to a human being at work can affect his or her experience of "well-being" or "morale" there, positively, negatively or in a way which has little lasting impact. This being so, we need to examine *every aspect of work life, as broadly*

---

* Using the statistical technique called "factor analysis" and inputting large amounts of survey data, groupings of work-life factors are generated. This happens when people respond similarly to each question in that factor, indicating that each question is measuring various aspects of the same factor.

as we can, in order to reach the drivers of morale amongst the workforce, and measure them.

Factors which affect everyone's morale

To make this view possible, we bring these aspects together into what we call "factors", or groupings which have both a common-sense reason to be together, and also a statistical one.* While this is not an all-inclusive list (factors and individual items are often examined based on the unique needs of an organization), major factors appropriate *for all members of the workforce* include:

- *Individual job and organization image:* This includes how people view their organization and their work; it can also include how they think others (such as customers or the community) see the organization. A typical issue covered here might also be whether the employee likes the organization enough to recommend it to others as a place to work, that is, to what extent is that person willing to be a positive ambassador or advocate? Creation of this image within the individual and collective mind of employees is determined by the "behavior" of the organization toward its employees, in its marketplace or sphere of influence and in its community. Ethics comes into play here, sometimes in a big way. Image is also determined by the other factors listed below and how the organization performs in each area.
- *Compensation and benefits:* Under this heading are reactions to external competitiveness and internal equity (fairness without regard to the external) of pay, and to the list of any and all benefits which the organization provides, such as supplemental health care, pension plans, etc. Pay and performance issues are also covered.
- *Career and development:* Here we find those aspects which relate to opportunity for advancement, fairness of the advancement process, hiring from within versus from outside, training and development opportunities in order to improve skills and knowledge, etc. It can also include whether the employee desires to stay in the organization.
- *Job security:* Does the employee feel secure in the job and about the organization's survival and development?

8

- *Communications:* Of all the information which comes to employees, which is most important? Is information credible? Is the *way* in which it is presented appropriate, interesting?
- *Productivity:* What things get in the way of the employee being productive? Is it lack of clear directions, poor or minimal training, management behavior, poorly designed workflow? Do some in the employee's workgroup carry much more weight, while others are allowed to drift along and do the minimum with no consequences?
- *Working conditions:* This can include physical working conditions, safety, tools and equipment; investment in quality office space, health facilities and related aspects.
- *Management and supervision:* How does the employee see his/her supervisor or team leader? Of all the things which supervisors are expected to do, does the supervisor accomplish them?* How about mid- and senior- management? What is their "image" with workers? Is there fairness of treatment by management/supervision? Or is there "favoritism", where better treatment and advantages flow based on "who you know"? When was the last time the employee had a "performance review" and how motivating and informative was it? Is it possible to "go beyond" the supervisor if there is a serious issue (does the so-called "open-door" policy translate into *actual practice*)?
- *Decision making:* This covers the level at which decisions are made, whether this level is appropriate or not; whether the decisions are of high quality, made with appropriate speed, etc.

Generally these factors are seen as being relevant to ALL employees. But there are other issues which are relevant to subsets of the workforce. Do we leave these out of the morale model? The answer is yes and no. Yes when we are looking at the *overall workforce*, because the factors above are relevant to everyone, no matter the function or the level in the organization. But some organizations want to focus on a specific group like their salesforce or management team; they wish to

---

* There is a long list of these which are usually examined in the morale measurement process, because they all impact morale. Examples of these include giving information to do the job, communicating about career opportunities, encouraging suggestions, planning work, setting expectations for performance, addressing performance problems and simply *listening* to employees when that is what is needed.

dig deeper into issues which affect their morale and which are not so relevant to everyone else. They should be able to look at this, and our model should account for it. Let's examine now what some of these factors are.

Factors which affect management morale

Generally speaking, management has a viewpoint which is different from that of the average employee. For example, there is usually more perspective of the competition, strategic strengths and weaknesses of their organization versus the competition, etc. The extent to which the organization functions well in these and other areas affects management morale. Some of these crucial management morale factors are:

- *Sense of direction:* Does management share a clear sense of the organization's mission? Are there clear goals and measurement processes in place to know if those goals are being reached?
- *Performance focus:* Is management held accountable for what they do? Are there consequences for success – and failure? Are managers held to a high standard of performance?
- *Speed and urgency:* These days business life moves extremely fast; does the organization act like a pacesetter or a slow follower? Is there a general sense of urgency in areas where there needs to be?
- *Leadership style and decision making:* Does management have a sense they are supported from above? Are they free to take independent innovative action, make customer-oriented improvements? Are management decisions made at the right level, or does every decision, no matter how small, have to "go to the top"? Are good decisions made and communicated, and does top management follow through on them?
- *Management development and promotion:* Are managers presented with opportunities for development of their skills and abilities? Are the most "people-capable" managers the ones who are promoted, or simply the ones who are most knowledgeable about the technical aspects of the function they are managing?
- *Management compensation:* Often there are special compensation plans in place to reward management; these might be stock options

(these also exist more and more at the non-management level); incentive plans, etc. How effective and competitive are they?

Factors which affect sales force morale

■ *Clarity of sales strategy, forecasts and goals:* Are sales people clear on the sales strategy which their organization follows? Do they have clear goals and objectives? Are their forecasts and goals realistic?
■ *Sales and marketing tools:* What types of sales and marketing tools are given to the salesforce? Are they useful and effective? Current?
■ *Customer focus; quality of service or product delivered to customer; quality of salesforce itself:* Does the salesforce see the organization as being oriented toward the customer, or perhaps more to the products it develops and produces? How does the salesforce perceive the quality of what it sells and how the organization follows through in after-sales service? Is there a general focus in sales on the quality aspect of everything they do? Does the salesforce see itself as strong versus the competition?
■ *Sales compensation issues:* Is sales compensation fair? Is it related to sales achievements in a way that is motivating?
■ *Sales and customer-service training:* Is this effective, frequent and comprehensive enough?
■ *Territory and teamwork issues:* Are territories handled in a fair way, as far as the salesforce is concerned? Do they make sense from a customer perspective? Do salespeople work as a team or are they protective of territories or functions to the detriment of the customer?
■ *Authority to meet customer needs:* Do the salesforce and customer service employees have the authority to take care of customer needs without going up the "chain of command"?

When we step back and consider it, any or all these factors are at work every day and can affect our morale there. A sense that a manager "plays favorites" can incense an individual who is not part of the "in" group. In a case with a positive outcome, an individual might feel very good about meeting goals and having a larger raise than others who have not met their goals. However, all of this does not happen by chance: leadership sets the tone of things, determines how the organization functions in all the areas above, and this brings us to our model of Morale (Figure 1):

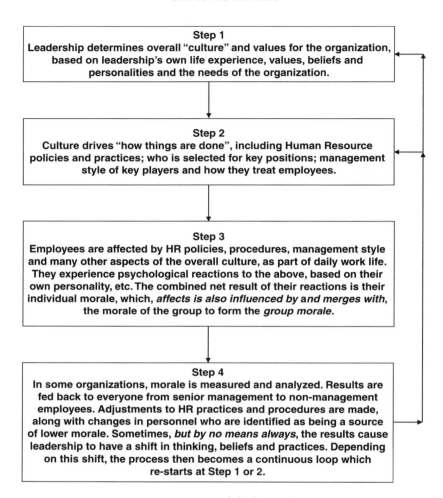

FIGURE 1 **Model of morale**

NOTES ON THE MORALE MODEL

■ *Step 1:* The best definition which we know of "corporate culture" is from the book of that same name first published in 1982:[6] [7] "the way we do things around here". Much of the selection of a cultural orientation can be unconscious, partly because many organization founders are people who are not aware of the underlying beliefs and value systems with which they have grown up and which they carry forward into the organization. To them, these opinions and beliefs are "common sense" and "normal".

Yet these unconscious beliefs often drive what these leaders select as a de facto "culture" (but not using that name). A frugal childhood often translates into a frugal company, linoleum instead of carpeting even for senior management offices, the absolute minimum of attention of "comfort" for any employees. One should never underestimate the effects (both positive and negative) of a powerful leader with a strong value system on the organization's culture, and it sometimes endures even long after that person has passed away. Stories are told which perpetuate this value system, with tag lines like "Fred would *never* have done that!!" The computer and electronics company Hewlett Packard (now HP) comes to mind: its powerful and incredibly successful people-oriented value system, generated very early on by its two founders, became known as "The HP Way".

Cultural orientation is also affected by the country in which an organization is situated, the type of industry in which it finds itself, or whether it is a non-profit such as a government or non-governmental organization like a police force or an international charity. Even within these categories there can be big cultural differences, such as that of a shareholder-owned power company compared to a state or local government-owned one. The types of people necessary to run and staff one of these organizations, and who will be attracted to them, can be quite different. The amount of regulation, necessary structure, history of the industry ... all have their cultural impact, which in turn can affect morale. However, management will always have an outsized impact on morale, at the top and at every level, regardless of these other influences. Dramatic positive cultural and morale changes can take place even in what some might think of as a "staid" company with a decades-long history of cultural stability, when the right steps are taken by the leadership.

■ *Step 2:* Human resources policies and procedures, the formal rules by which organizations conduct their people-oriented affairs, therefore do not come into place by accident. Nor do the less formalized, day-to-day behaviors of management and supervision toward employees, or even employees toward each other. They are driven by the momentum of the culture (stated or not) to perpetuate itself and its effect on people and how they should be treated. If this sounds like the culture takes on a life of its own, that is correct, it often does! Try changing the culture at an organization and you will find out that this is often a multi-year, time- and resource-consuming task, which does not always end in success.

- *Step 3:* Translated from bureaucratic-sounding processes like "HR policies and procedures", the implementation of these becomes very real to employees: it determines how much they are paid, how often their performance is reviewed, what kinds of opportunities for advancement are available and whether these positions are filled from outside or from talent which is available in-house. The list goes on and on, and to each of these there is a *reaction*. What is interesting here is that our model sets out a feedback loop from the individual to the group, so that group morale is not only the aggregate of individual but also affected, perhaps changed, by individual morale. Individual morale is also changed by group morale, as the model shows. For an example of the individual>group effect, an employee who feels she has been badly treated by a team leader will most likely share this with her team; the team might have been feeling moderately positive about the leader but this new information changes their collective mind, and morale shifts to the downside among them. Also important here is the fact that one work situation does not affect all individuals in precisely the same way: personality mediates the effect. One person's stress can be another's stimulation and excitement, for example. Having said that, commonalities of reactions are such that the group can have, and often does have, a group reaction to events at work.

- *Step 4:* This is a feedback loop which is the subject of much of this book. The system makes change in morale possible by measuring how it is doing and feeding back that information to the top (at the beginning) and then to everyone. Of course, the culture may not be one which "wishes"* to take this step. Measurement of morale can and does expose the "dark side" and what is not working. Not everyone wants to hear this and if that group includes the CEO or powerful member of top management, it will not happen. These are the people who will say, when asked if they ever survey their employees to measure morale: "Why open Pandora's Box?" The simple answer is this: *"Because measuring it doesn't create the issues that this comes up with, they're already there and affecting your organization in significant ways!"* On the positive side, the fact that the organization is doing an analysis of its morale means that it is already in the group of those which at least has the courage to

---

* We don't mean to anthropomorphize culture too much, but sometimes it really does seem like it has a life of its own.

look at itself, and hopefully act on what it finds. Most of those senior management individuals who have no desire to in any way improve morale will not embark on this process in the first place.

Since we say this is a loop, are we saying that *in some cases* Step 4 can actually *affect* Step 1? Can the result of a morale measurement process such as a survey really change the *core values, personalities and experiences of top management* such that they will make the shifts necessary to change things in Step 2? Well, it certainly affects experience; any consultant in this area will tell you stories of a CEO, division or country manager shocked into humility by the loud sound of the workforce talking back to them. Not to overdramatize, but this can really be something to behold, and a chance for real change for both that individual and that part of the organization for which they are responsible. On the other hand, sometimes it is not necessary or possible to change someone's values or experience, beliefs and behavior: it is easier to find a new person with the values and personality and experience which is more closely aligned to creating a high morale workplace, and this is indeed what often happens.

CHAPTER 2

HOW DO ORGANIZATIONS
MEASURE MORALE?

We have a question for you:

**Its Monday morning in Beijing, London or Sydney; do you
really know how your employees there are doing?**

We chose three places so that you could pick the furthest one from
your current location; a far away place makes it more difficult to
know all that is happening, because even with communications at
the speed of light, information still degrades with time and distance.
But the question is also valid for any location where you operate,
even if it is close to where you work, or actually in the same building.
We could ask it as easily for Birmingham, England or Birmingham,
Alabama. We can ask it for a huge multinational corporation, or for
a small rural hospital. Do you *really* know how your employees are
doing?

So let's assume the answer is in the affirmative and you do know
your employees' mood, their *morale*; we have some more questions
for you.

How do you know?
From whom did you learn it?
Do those from whom you learned it represent the whole organization?
When did you last find out? Could there have been a shift since then?
Are you SURE that what you know is true?
What are the consequences if what you think is true, is not?

Consider a true situation, condensed into one from countless similar
experiences we have had in organizations, with a little tongue-in-
cheek added for effect: a CEO arrives at a subsidiary location on his

yearly "Managing by Walking Around"* tour. He and his small entourage step onto the elevator and find Jones already occupying it. Jones is immediately engaged in conversation by the CEO:

> *CEO*: I'm Smith, pleased to meet you.
> *Jones*: Yes sir. I've seen you on the video presentations we get around here, pleased to meet you too, I'm Jones.
> *CEO*: So how long have you worked here?
> *Jones*: 10 years sir.
> *CEO*: And how are things going for you here?
> *Jones*: Very well thanks sir, never felt better at a job.
> *CEO*: Do you think most people like working here Jones?
> *Jones*: Oh yes sir, I think they really do.
> *CEO*: So do you work well as a team?
> *Jones*: Yes we do sir, I think our quarterly numbers demonstrate that.

The lift arrives at the 25th floor and the CEO and entourage step out, thanking Jones as they go. The CEO is feeling good; some positive information has come to him from one of the longer tenured members of staff. He is encouraged by what he has heard and is feeling good about the morale in the subsidiary. But he is *completely misguided* in his conclusion. He has conducted what we call an *"ambush survey"* (not of course limited to lifts) and has made two crucial methodological mistakes plus one unwarranted assumption:

1. His sample size is 1, not in any way representing the whole, and yet he has generalized from this to the whole population of the subsidiary.
2. His data was collected under extreme duress, i.e., the fear engendered by the situation of being with one's *boss's boss's boss*, instead of under absolute confidentiality (which would allow for truthful expression).
3. There are any number of ways in which the subsidiary can meet its numbers, some of which involve anything but engendering high levels of morale. Indeed those methods could be destroying long term morale while showing short-term results.

---

* A phrase first used by Peters and Waterman in their 1982 classic 'In Search of Excellence'.

Even if he were to expand his sample to half the total population of the subsidiary or more, his data would still be suspect for the same reason as in 2 above. His data is therefore *completely invalid and his conclusions unwarranted*. At this point he has no idea of the real morale situation in the subsidiary.

Maybe the ambush survey sounds absurd, but many individuals in organizations use it, in one form or another. It can be conducted by phone of course, and often is. *Its particular feature is the big difference in "rank" between the participants.*

So what does one do to find out "what's going on?" Many methods exist, each with their strengths and weaknesses. By examining each one, we can see how they rate on our question list above. We will start with the less formal, less specific formats, by which we mean those which are not designed to gather large amounts of information from significant percentages of the workforce, or the whole employee population. The informal methods are part of the ebb and flow of everyday life in the organization, and are often quite spontaneous. Then we will graduate to the more structured methods for gathering data.

MEASURING MORALE: INFORMAL METHODS

Method 1: The casual chat

Probably the most common method for measuring organizational morale, the casual chat between team leader or manager and employees can be a superb way of "keeping one's ear to the ground" and finding out what is going on. We differentiate this from the ambush survey because the latter has unique characteristics which are not shared by the typical casual chat, primarily the rank difference between the "surveyor" and "surveyed", and element of fear created by that difference. This is because the average employee does not see the CEO or any other member of senior management every day, and in most medium to large size organizations even once every year. Also, in spite of our caustic characterization of a CEO skimming the surface with a scared "subordinate", and drawing erroneous conclusions from his experience, many CEOs or members of senior management are quite capable of not intimidating "lower" level employees. In spite of that skill on their part, however, it is questionable as to whether they still hear the truth as to what is happening in the organization. Our survey data bear this out: many organizations' top management teams, from large and small organizations, have been shocked as to what surveys have revealed.

In smaller organizations, owners or members of senior management are often talking with so-called "line" employees regularly on a casual basis. In the larger setting, among smaller subgroups, casually chatting becomes easier, and fear is reduced. This is where much valuable information is gathered by such discourses, between mid level management, first level supervision and employees. In many cases, these people socialize together outside the workplace, trust is formed and information can be more safely shared.

> Strengths: If some trust is there, managers can easily and quickly have a limited-perspective view of the organization this way. As a potentially open-ended method of gathering information, new and valuable material can be gathered which helps management at least find out where further, more reliable, enquiry might be needed.

> Weaknesses: Without trust, information will be carefully screened before it is shared, and much will be hidden; and with a poor listener who only wants to hear certain things, even if new and valuable information is shared, it will not be heard. Across a divide of more than one rank level, information gathered this way will be quite suspect.

Method 2: The "open door"

Perhaps you wonder why we put this in quotes: it's for a good reason. Many say that their door is open, but is it really? Talk can be cheap; saying "my door is always open" sounds good to employees; but really having an open door means having to devote time and energy when one might not have either at the end of a long day, when someone appears who really, really needs to talk. For those who *really* practice this, it is a lifeline which employees appreciate and can be done at the local level, or even in a much larger setting. Sir Richard Branson is famous for giving out his home and mobile phone numbers to employees of his Virgin airline, because he would rather hear about problems from employees than from customers. The "open door" can therefore be virtual, and worldwide.

Again, all depends on trust and listening, and this is where the "open door" can break down: just one situation where an employee uses the open door and a negative consequence occurs, can be devastating. Over the years we have heard of many cases of direct firings by the so-called open door manager, or of other managers or employees being informed of what someone had said about them. None of these had positive consequences.

Strengths : Gives employees a sense that they can "skip rank", if necessary, to report on difficulties ranging all the way from sexual harassment or rampant favoritism to minor office or workplace issues. As such, it provides a source of protection for employees and can keep these negative things from happening or quickly fix them if they do.

Weaknesses: Often not implemented, just stated. Requires real time and attention commitments which some are not willing to make. Vulnerable to abuse by insensitive managers, who should avoid even offering this service (problem: they do not always know who they are).

MEASURING MORALE: FORMAL METHODS

Method 3: Group/team meetings (not including self-directed work teams)

As we move into the more formally structured methods of identifying morale issues, we're referencing here the type of meetings set up to talk specifically about morale and/or operational issues; many organizations have these once a week, at the departmental or workgroup level, and they provide valuable information when done right. Again, all depends on the skill and listening abilities of management, the trust which has been developed, etc. Are some people allowed to dominate the conversation? (The "attention hogs", we will visit them later.) Running a small group well is something people can study for years, while others seem to have the "knack" for it. Even when run very well, however, it is intimidating for someone to really bring up serious issues, like those mentioned above, in front of people they might see every day. What if the problem lies with the person running the meeting?

Strengths: Allows employees to share with their workgroup; permits them to see that others might share their concerns, frustrations, etc.

21

Gives the group a chance to develop solutions to many issues, develops a sense of teamwork and empowerment.

Weaknesses: Not always a safe environment to raise sensitive issues; team members or the leader themselves, especially if management, can be the issue one wants to, but cannot necessarily, discuss. Can be manipulated or dominated by "attention hogs" if such people are not controlled by peer pressure or a strong leader.

Method 4: Self-directed work teams

These exist for several reasons, most of all to cut layers of organizational bureaucracy, speed decision making and empower people to make decisions at the "local" level. They solve a lot of issues themselves, often dispensing with HR completely, and using peer pressure to make things run smoothly, dealing with performance issues, absences, etc. As such they can be extremely effective, and do not suffer from many of the weaknesses found in the traditional employee meeting format. We will examine evidence for the performance of self-directed work teams in the next chapter.

Strengths: With no management presence, teams are free to bring up and discuss all kinds of issues without the influence this normally has on the potential for candid discussion, openness, etc.

Weaknesses: Not everyone is comfortable discussing all issues, even in a "safe" peer-to-peer environment. As a result, some concerns within the work team, even if self-directed, can only be identified in a more confidential manner.

Method 5: "360" Reviews

The 360 Review is an interesting HR innovation which extends the performance review process from its usual limited "top down" boss-subordinate domain to something much more comprehensive: all team members are reviewed by all others, including the manager or team leader. This means the latter individual will receive an evaluation from people who work for him/her. As an exercise in workplace democracy, this is a huge move forward and a source of valuable information. Of course it can also threaten the status of an insecure manager, in a major way, which is one of the reasons why it is done. Egos* must be left at the door, or they are in danger of being crushed.

Since the evaluations are carried out in a confidential way, an employee does not know who is saying the nice things or voicing those criticisms: however it can be quite easy to guess. The trick here is to have sufficient training in the process and some clear rules as to how it should be carried through: no attempts to find out who said what, no confrontations after the fact, etc. Theoretically, it should come as no surprise to a team leader or manager when the results come out; after all, if they have an "open door" they will already know everything that is being said, right? Forgive us a wry smile at this thought: as we mentioned above, the "open door" can often look like a locked bank safe door when one tries to walk through it. The outcome of a 360 review is therefore quite a shock, especially for the first time, not only to managers but also team members who receive peer reviews. If the process is handled well though, these uncomfortable moments can lead to insight, learning and a forward move which would be impossible without this information. The "learning organization" does, after all, depend on thousands and thousands of these situations. Far be it for us to suggest that there is not a balance of positive information in this process as well: it is rewarding indeed to know how one's peers see positive contributions and changes which one has made, etc. This reinforces such behavior for the future and provides bonding for team members.

Interestingly, technology from the social networking arena has been brought to the 360 review process: as *BusinessWeek* reported in March 2009,[1] a company called Rypple lets people post short (maximum 140 characters) questions rather like those on the phenomenally successful Twitter program, requesting feedback on their performance. According to Rypple, as reported in the magazine,

---

* The term "ego" is used here to mean a separate false identity which an individual builds up as a defense mechanism from childhood. Egos can take on a life of their own, even change and completely take over the personality of their host. As a false identity they are by nature fragile, and require constant reinforcement and protection. Their host, in this case the manager, often spends a great deal of energy defending them; the organization's power structure allows this to continue but this is threatened by the break in this structure represented by a 360 degree review.

an astounding 66 percent of these requests are from managers rather than from individual employees. We would venture a guess that the type of manager making this request might have a higher morale team than one who does not.

Method 6: The focus group

A focus group dedicated to exploring morale is a meeting which has specific goals, typically to examine a pre-designed list of issues and open discussion for other topics which are of importance to the group. Many focus groups are run by external consultants but are also an important tool for internal HR consulting contributors to look at issues like perceptions of benefits, etc. If part of an employee survey, the focus group is often used to develop a sense of which issues should be covered in the questionnaire. However, the groups can also be used effectively without preceding a survey, especially when a specific topic is examined in depth (as in the benefits example). Important factors here include

- Making the group representative of the larger entity which it represents, in order to be able to generalize views on the issues back to that larger entity.
- Confidentiality, in that participants are asked not to discuss outside the group about things which have been covered inside (of course, being a meeting of *human beings*, this is not always possible!)
- Need for a skilled facilitator, in order to steer the group to the task at hand, keep "attention hogs" and other species like "complainers"* from dominating the conversation and controlling the issues.

Strengths: The group can deliver extremely valuable information to the organization; if trust is built and the group carefully steered, participants will open up and pour out things they want to change, improve, etc. The feeling of having a "voice" can be very intense and is often greatly appreciated. Even if the group keeps its promise of not sharing actual content with other employees outside the group, the process itself will be shared and can be a big

---

* Complaining can be an important function in a focus group, within limits; the complaint may contain extremely valuable information. We are not referring to complaints per se, but to a type of person who makes a full time profession of it; a skilled facilitator knows the difference and how to manage the group when one or more such persons is present.

plus in terms of how people see the organization's willingness to listen.

Weaknesses: Selecting participants for the focus group is usually done on a fairly informal basis, not using scientific sampling techniques, which are often not practical in an organization; the extent to which the group really represents the whole therefore comes into question. The data are also collected in anecdotal form, which, although useful, has its limits. Depending on the skill of the facilitator, participants may not feel free to open up about key issues, and they may also fear (correctly or incorrectly) that bringing up controversial subjects in front of their peers will create negative consequences for them later. An in-house facilitator could exacerbate that concern.

Method 7: The employee opinion survey

This is the mother of all data gathering techniques in the area of morale, which is why we have already mentioned it several times. By now, most employees in the United States and many in Europe and Asia will have experienced this, in one of the organizational settings which make up their career. It is a process which, **when carried out correctly**, generates huge amounts of valuable information. The process itself – just doing the survey, and not counting the data or changes which are generated – can provide an employee-relations return on investment far greater in intensity than the focus group. Because of its importance, we will spend considerable time here on it. Typical features include

- Total census instead of sampling: this means that, typically, all employees are invited to complete a survey. Sampling is done in some organizations, but as consultants we recommended against it as the main data collection tool because of the need to give *everyone* a sense that their opinion is important, not just 10 percent of the workforce. We would suggest that, if necessary, sampling be limited to a quick "flash" look at issues in-between larger scale surveys.
- Confidentiality: by limiting aggregated data feedback for groups less than a fixed number, for example eight respondents, no individual is identified.
- Use of outside consultants: this is often done because of the need to demonstrate to employees that their data are secure, offsite and that

the consultants control the data flow back to the organization such that the promise of confidentiality can be kept. In addition, external specialized firms often have

– comparison databases ("benchmarks")
– specialized software with which to "mine" the data
– experience in running the logistics of the survey, which can be quite complicated and are very important
– experience in interpreting the data, often misinterpreted by those with less experience, at significant cost to the organization.

■ Data in numeric form: this simple fact means groups can be compared with each other and with their previous results, sometimes over many years; they can be compared to external groups which have answered the same questions, perhaps within the same industry. *In none of the other methods of identifying morale issues, which we have discussed in this Chapter, is this possible.*

The strengths and weaknesses of various forms of data gathering for the measurement of morale are shown below in Table 1.

As our Table below shows, the employee survey solves many problems which are created by other methods of gathering information about an organization's morale. Note that the survey is:

■ The *ONLY* method which generates numeric data.
■ The *ONLY* method to mix both numeric and anecdotal data. By having an open-ended section (or sections) in the questionnaire, employees can also write in comments on anything they wish. This means the survey is open to data which is not structured into the actual questions, and new and often valuable data is generated this way.
■ The *ONLY* method to provide confidentiality; whether the employees believe this or not (which is another issue based on past experiences with surveys and other factors like the use of outside consultants to completely control the data), it is available if certain conditions are met. Information collected under conditions of confidentiality is far more valuable than that which is not.
■ The *ONLY* method to provide such depth of analysis. With a questionnaire typically containing 100 or more items, plus one or more open-ended sections, one has a far more in-depth look into the organization than with other data collection methods. This is why we sometimes call it an organizational MRI or CT Scan. A one-hour

TABLE 1 Summary: Methods of gathering morale information

	Sample or 100% census?	Generalizable to the whole?	Anecdotal Or numeric?	Structured or new information possible?	Confidential?	Allows for in-depth study of issues?
Ambush survey	Sample (small)	No	Anecdotal	New information limited by fear factor	No	No
Casual chat	Sample (small)	No	Anecdotal	New information, but limited	No	No
Group/team meeting	Sample (very limited)	No	Anecdotal	New information, but limited	No	Yes, can do over time
Self-directed group	Sample (very limited)	No*	Anecdotal	New information, but limited	No	Yes, can do over time
360 Review	Sample	No	Usually anecdotal	Mainly structured, some new information	Often limited due to small group size	Yes, can do over time
Focus group	Sample (usually limited)◆	Limited	Anecdotal	New information, but limited	No	Yes, but limited by time
Employee survey	Typically 100% census*	Yes	Both	Both	Yes	Yes

* The self-directed work group can generate a lot of valuable information concerning its own area; indeed, that is part of its value and the reason why it often replaces management and support functions like HR through its own activities; however we refer here to the ability to generalize to the whole organization.

◆ If multiple focus groups are conducted and they are structured to truly represent the organization's demographics as a whole, they can generate information which, although still derived from a sample, can be quite generalizable to the whole.

* Some organizations carry out 100 percent census surveys every year to 18 months and sample surveys in-between.

focus group would tire if asked to talk about all these issues, and would run out of time long before reaching the 100-item level, whereas a survey can be completed in 20–30 minutes.

"OPINION" VS. "ATTITUDE"

Most people will have heard the phrase "Employee Attitude Survey", which is still quite widely used. We prefer the word "Opinion" because "Attitude" can have a certain negative connotation in popular language (as in: "he really has an *attitude* today" or "she has an *attitude* problem"). In neither of these cases would the word "Opinion" be used. Besides, organization-wide surveys are often presented to employees with phrases like "What's Your Opinion?" or "Your Opinion Counts". Again the word "attitude" would not work for this purpose.

Goals of the survey process

Most organizations which take the path to surveying their employees have multiple goals:

1. They want quantitative data on morale in order to know "how employees are doing" in their organization.
2. Often they have surveyed before and wish to know how things have changed since the last survey.
3. They sometimes wish to be compared to other organizations, such as those in their industry, or ones that have been identified as having "best practices"; this data will make it possible.
4. They wish to identify management issues which need to be addressed; some of these are already evident to senior management, and some will come to light only as a result of the survey. These might include the performance of managers themselves in dealing with their "troops".
5. They wish to have a basis for action which is based on reality, not on rumor, gossip, or other suspicious and unreliable data sources.
6. They wish to test such things as values statements or other verbal representations of organization culture, to see if they are really true, or no more than words in the annual report or employee newspaper.

28

7. They wish to give employees a "voice", and to demonstrate in action that employee opinions are not only important, but that action will be taken to correct serious issues identified in the survey.

Reading this list, it is apparent that this is no ordinary process; in fact, many HR consultants (which include ourselves) will tell listeners that *hardly anything which can be done in an organization, on the people side of the business, can compare to the power of the process and content of an employee survey.* These benefits accrue when all aspects are handled with care and skill. Of course, anything with such power and influence which is mishandled can result in (and we choose the word carefully) a *catastrophic* employee-relations situation: a complete loss of faith in management and unwillingness to ever participate in such an exercise again. So we will warn you here: it is far better to not go ahead with this if you do not plan to carry it through correctly. Better to be at zero than minus fifty!

In-house versus outside?

Early on, the organization will have to make the decision to go with an outside consultant or do the work in-house. This decision is already made by those large organizations which keep in-house teams for this purpose, although our perception is that this is a smaller and smaller number over time. Even if a specialized team isn't already on board, some organizations might decide to form a team from skilled in-house individuals. As much as we might be tempted to make the case for *never* doing this, and argue for job security for consultants such as ourselves, there are certain benefits which accrue to conducting a survey in house:

- Cost can be an issue; in-house people are already on the payroll.
- Control of the process is another issue and especially control of the data, which might be seen as too sensitive to allow outside the organization
- The organization might be able to find materials such a generic questionnaires on the Internet, for survey purposes, and if it looks hard enough, some national "norms", or benchmark data, against which it can compare itself.

On the other hand (and you might have suspected the list of benefits for outside consultants would be longer!), most organizations of a certain size (starting at 100 or so employees) seem to get external help in conducting a survey. They do this because:

- Outsiders can promise and keep promises of confidentiality. The perception among the employees is that their opinions are kept in "trust" or safekeeping by the outside firm. When trust has been broken in the organization through whatever situation, this is especially important. Even when this has not happened, the perception (an important word in this business) is that it's better to keep the data safe on the outside. An example of this might be: the CEO comes to the consultant and asks for a postsurvey data breakout for a group of 6 people in a sensitive area. The consultant turns this request down because promises have been made to employees that only groups of 8 or more will be identified in aggregate. Would an in-house person be able to handle this pressure or would he/she cave in? In one case the consultant risks losing a client, in the second an in-house person risks losing his or her job.
- Specialized software: nowadays a great deal of survey software and services is available which can doubtless aggregate the raw data for you. Going deeper into the data is, however, essential if one is to make full use of it. This requires specialized software which is not available off-the-shelf (we had to write our own) and an external consultant will be more likely to have developed this.

Methodology of the employee opinion survey

- *Planning*

  At this stage decisions are made as to whether to go with an in-house survey or an externally conducted version. Decisions are also made as to total census versus sample, with census being the overwhelming favorite. Logistical issues are planned with the consultants, sometimes involving questionnaire distribution choices such as group "paper and pencil" sessions or Internet distribution, which is increasingly prevalent. Language needs may come into the discussion here, as well.

■ *Input for questionnaire: (1) focus groups*

If this is an ongoing process, where the survey has been repeated every 18 months or so (an average period between surveys), a questionnaire will already exist. Making big changes to this will be counterproductive because comparisons with prior data will not then be possible. However, some new issues might have emerged since the last survey and may need to be addressed. Whether a follow-on to a prior series of surveys or a new survey process, the need for information leading to survey questions is essential at this point, and most organizations turn to the focus group. The exception is the organization where only very minor questionnaire changes are necessary.

If a new questionnaire is constructed, it will probably be based on some tried and true questions which go back many years and are handed down from one generation of consultants to the next. These have two big advantages: they have a lot of external benchmark data against which one can compare oneself; secondly, they have been "tested" many times for what is called "content validity" (meaning, does the question really measure what it purports to measure?). Such testing is also carried out in focus groups, where participants are shown questions and asked to comment on the meaning they attribute to them. This is then checked against the meaning which is intended by the question.

Regular focus groups are used to create new questionnaires or very large changes on an existing document. New questions can be pre-tested with one or more groups, as needed.

■ *Input for questionnaire: (2) management interviews*

While the focus group input is valuable, management interviews are usually also conducted. These can be one-on-one at the senior and mid levels or group sessions starting at mid level to first line supervisory, to account for the need to tap into the knowledge of more people. They serve the purpose of not only gaining management perspective on morale issues in general but also covering issues which should and do find their way into the questionnaire. These issues often go beyond the normal understanding of morale, such as clarity of strategic direction as perceived by management itself, and cultural issues such as values, mission, etc. If an outside firm is hired to conduct the survey, a consultant will also want to fully get to know the organization, its competition and position *vis à vis* that competition, its history and other factors which will help in *understanding and interpreting the data*. Typically senior members of management are first asked to describe the state of morale in the organization as a whole, and in their own area of responsibility.

Design of the questionnaire

Questionnaire content is driven by the input from employees in focus groups, the management interviews and core questions which are asked in most surveys. In this way, the organization will have access to data on unique issues which are central to its mission, or simply of interest, but which may not be so important to others; it will also be able to use questions which have been heavily pre-tested with millions of employees around the world, and have been found useful in many different settings. These questions often tie in to larger databases (often broken down by geography and organizational/industry type), which may be available to the survey team. Several issues are very important here:

- The survey must be *understandable* to all those whom it will reach; you want the response to the question to be about the issues which that question addresses, not based on the respondent's educational level. If there is any issue about this, questions should be pre-tested in the way we have discussed before, with focus groups representing all educational level of employees who will eventually take the full survey.
- If new questions are designed, great care must be made to ensure that they do not *"lead" the respondent to a specific response*. Many times when one mentions that one works in the survey business, people will spontaneously respond: "Oh, those questions are fixed and you can prove anything you want". This may be true in the case of the question: "Have you stopped beating your spouse?", but it should never be true on your employee survey.
- Questionnaires nearly always contain crucial "demographic" sections which typically identify such items as
  - Age
  - Sex
  - Time on the job
  - Larger organizational unit (functional unit, etc.)

32

- Smaller organizational unit
- Subgroups down to about 8–10 minimum employees[*]
- Organizational level (top management, mid management, supervisory, non-management, etc.)
- Job type (sales, clerical, manufacturing, etc.)
- Larger geographic location (like France)
- Geographic sublocations (Provence, Brittany, etc.)

Distribution of the survey

In the very late 1990s, distribution of questionnaires started to move from the classic system of bringing the employees together in groups to complete the survey together, using paper and pencil. The newer technology of Internet distribution became popular for a number of reasons, but also presented serious issues of confidentiality, which we believe may still be something of an issue. In the end though, Internet distribution has won the hearts and minds of many survey users. Let's examine the two methods in terms of their strengths and weaknesses.

1. Paper and pencil survey in a group setting: Strengths

Bringing everyone together in a group can create an atmosphere of fun for a group. We have mentioned before the employee relations "plus" of doing a survey. This is an event which adds to that positive benefit. In an ideal scenario, employees are invited to attend the meeting, which is voluntary (compulsory surveys are useless and will yield invalid data). Perhaps coffee and doughnuts are served, and an introductory speech is made by the facilitator (either an in-house person from HR[♦] or sometimes a member of the outside consulting team).

---

[*] In order to reassure employees that their confidentiality will be protected, groups of less than 8 persons are not usually broken out under any circumstances. Without this reassurance, the data could be skewed by a fear factor and would therefore be far less reliable as a measure of employees' real views.

[♦] An "outsider" is more often used than a member of the team being surveyed; the projection of not just the image but the reality of confidentiality is important. Local conditions often prevail as to who is perceived as most trustworthy. Often having the outside consultant distribute all questionnaires in this way proves too costly, given the size of some organizations.

The speech can stress, in person, the fact that the survey is confidential, that no one in groups of less than 8 persons will be identified, etc. It would also stress that the company wants their own view, not that of their neighbor; this is in no way like being told not to cheat in a school "test", it is a very different message about the uniqueness and value of each person's responses. Indeed the word "test" is often brought up in order to stress the differences, and say what the survey is not. Questions can be answered and commitments made as to the fact that *feedback **will** happen and all employees will see and hear the results of the survey for their area.* The survey is then distributed, 20–30 minutes or so passes until everyone is complete and all questionnaires are collected and sent *offsite as soon as possible* for processing.

2. Paper and pencil survey in a group setting: Weaknesses

The primary weakness of this method is the time it takes to process the data and get back to management and the employees with the results. Periods of 4–6 weeks were common, and the Internet methodology has made users intolerant of anything less than almost immediate turnaround. There are other things than can make this method less desirable, such as the (rare) loss of questionnaires in the shipping or data processing stages, etc.

3. Internet distribution: Strengths

The main advantage has already been mentioned above: speed! It is possible to have almost real-time data from a survey that is conducted via the Internet, and these days, who does not want that? Everything the Internet and mobile phone technology (which can also be used for surveys) has done for us has increased the speed with which we can work. We went from "snail mail" to e-mail; from dialing phone numbers, waiting for the phone to ring and perhaps leaving a message to instant messaging or texting. It makes a lot of sense but we are still left with a few questions:

4. Internet distribution: Possible weaknesses

When this was first introduced, we initially recommended that clients avoid this method for one very good reason: in order to ensure that respondents do not complete the survey more than once, there has to be a system for identifying that individual. The system which does that has to allow only one response to an "invitation" sent to your e-mail address or give you a unique "PIN" code to use up front or has to put a "cookie" on your computer after the survey has been taken. Whichever way is used, the "system" knows who you are. Consider this conversation we had with a survey software vendor, which illustrates the "Catch 22" nature of this issue.

Vendor: With the option we provide, each email address can take the survey only once
Us: And if they respond from more than one address?
Vendor: No, you will need to send them the email invitation to their email address
Us: If there is no invitation, its not possible to respond?
Vendor: Correct
Us: Do you ever get feedback that employees don't like to be so completely identified? I mean it's different than a customer survey, this is their job.
Vendor: In that case you will need to use anonymous surveys.
But with anonymous survey, respondents can answer the survey more than once.

If you complete, say, a political survey today on your laptop while sitting at home or in a café, you will find that when you try to go back and do it again, that is not possible. The system has identified you and made sure that you cannot spoil and invalidate its survey! The problem with this in the context of your organizational morale survey is that you must promise complete, 100 percent confidentiality, or your results will be invalidated by the bias due to concerns that respondents can be identified. Will they pour out their real issues to you when they are thinking that this is so? Absolutely not! You will receive only the most sanitized version of their feelings.

Consultants in the field say they have now found ways to both promise confidentiality and access the power and speed of Internet distribution. But the question remains:

*How do you ensure an employee has only participated once in the survey without identifying that person **in any way** which would affect their sense of complete confidentiality?*

One way to check on this is to look at the response rate to the survey: that would certainly be a casualty if employees felt very concerned indeed that they could be identified. At the same time though, there could be more subtle effects of employees who find themselves in this situation: they might still do the survey, but would make small but significant changes to their responses in the areas where they have the strongest negative feelings. Clearly this is not a good thing, it degrades the data. We believe more research needs to be done in this area to ensure that methods are truly perceived as 100 percent confidential by employees. A simple question on the survey might be added for example, asking if that is the case. But what if those who felt threatened by lack of confidentially due to the Internet distribution had already decided not to participate? Then the question would be completed only by those who already felt more safe, and their response would be invalid in terms of representing the whole organization.

Another possible area of concern with this methodology is that the employee might be allowed to complete the survey on her own time, including at home. This is a serious issue because at home another family member might pitch in and give their views, prompted or not. This would influence the respondent to give a different response than that which she might have given in a group session with her peers. Finally, reading the instructions about confidentiality alone at one's desk is quite different from hearing those words in a group meeting and having a chance to ask questions. For this reason, some organizations begin the process with a group meeting, then ask employees to go off and complete the survey at their workstation, within a given period of time.

One way or another, these are key issues if one wants to maximize the usefulness of morale data, and they keep some organizations doing things the "old fashioned way" with paper and pencil, in spite of its speed disadvantages.

Response rates

The response rate you receive from your workforce when they participate in an opinion survey is a crucial piece of data in its own right. What is the message they are sending to you if they refuse to participate in a voluntary process which most employees in most organizations seem to enthusiastically enjoy? Three possible messages come to mind:

We did this before and nothing happened. We aren't going to give you a chance to do that to us again.
We did this before and people were identified when you said they would not be. We aren't ....etc.
We never did this before but we don't trust what you say about confidentiality and our expectations for you actually something with this are close to zero; we will not take part.

In all three cases you have received some bad results even from those who did not take part. Perhaps the data you received from those who did decide to take part confirm this, perhaps they don't. It's all a question of how many decide not to participate. Typical response rates for our surveys averaged 85 percent, and that included worldwide programs in 34 languages and well over 10,000 participants. When one thinks about it, it is quite extraordinary that almost 9 in 10 employees in an organization would take the time and the trouble to do this in a voluntary way. It confirms what they say in the surveys we collected, that nothing piques their interest, in terms of communications, more than "the results of this survey".*

So what would we consider a bad response rate? Certainly 50 percent would be nothing to be proud of and would have serious consequences for you lower down the organization. But before explaining why, we need a quick primer on creating a scientifically valid sample. It's called *random stratified sampling*, and what it means is that you need to randomly select people from each age group, race group, time-on-the-job group, geographic location group, etc. ("strata") which exists in your organization, in proportion to the extent they are represented there. This is what pollsters do when trying to figure out if Labour, Liberals or Conservatives are ahead in UK elections: since they can't call all 60 million UK residents, they call 1000 people who have been randomly selected from the different

---

* Of course people may feel that pressure of work precludes them from being able to do the survey. Organizations take care of this by allowing sufficient time (for an Internet survey) or bringing workgroups together on organization time to complete the survey. Indeed, the latter is a message that 'we take this seriously enough that we ask you to come and do this now and not on your own time'.

"strata". In this way the pollsters can extrapolate (within a so-called margin of error created by the process) to the whole of the United Kingdom.

- Here is how this works assuming a 50 percent rate: the first question would be whether the 50 percent is randomly distributed throughout the organization. If so, then you have essentially allowed your employees to create a sample for your survey, albeit involuntarily and with far less control over your sampling process than one would want. This is hardly "random stratified sampling" at its finest.
- If you are lucky and a fair degree of randomness is the case, the results could be generalized to represent the whole. But only for the whole, and that is where things become more difficult. As one moves down the organization, the "sample" which has been created for you by the low response rate becomes less and less random for lower level, smaller groups, and they will not be able to have any valid data delivered to them.

The first problem created for you by a low response rate is therefore lack of data at lower levels, where managers might be very eager indeed to see how their group is doing. This defeats the purpose of the survey, at that level. However, if you have trust issues from a previous survey or from even being able to do one for the first time, you have more work do to.

Here are the options for the low response environment:

1. Do it right this time and demonstrate a "new beginning" for this type of process and the trust level in the organization. Go out of your way to communicate honestly, candidly, all results. Ensure absolute, total confidentiality of the process.
2. Wait to repair things before you try to survey. This can take a while, depending on the prior history. It also might not be palatable because you want the morale data now. But it is better to have valid data than data which gives you a false impression of what is happening.

When faced with a low response to a survey, clients would often ask us whether those who did not respond were somehow different to those who did. Perhaps, they asked, non-responders were so happy that they thought things could not possibly be improved by a morale survey process. This is by definition a very difficult question to answer, since they did not respond. An e-mail sent after the survey asking them why they didn't respond (assuming they could be identified in some way, something which would be against the spirit and promises of the program) would surely put your survey process back one generation of employees! So the answer has to come anecdotally, and over the years one hears that trust and fear of identification and also apathy created by low morale were the main culprits. Interestingly then, the very thing which you are trying to measure – morale – is going to affect the response to the measurement.

If you have a solid response rate, which we would put at 75–80 percent or more, you will have no reason to doubt the data for most levels. Be careful however, even where overall participation is high: the response for smaller groups may be well below the organization average. By following the "rule of 8" minimum display of data, you should avoid most issues of confidentiality, but there is more to consider: taking a hypothetical group of 15 persons with only a 40 percent response rate (6 people), that data would not be broken out under the rule of 8. But even a group of 16 with a 50 percent response rate is tricky: do the 8 who responded, really represent the whole? Also, in an organization with an 80 percent response, why did that group only respond at 50 percent? Most likely, there are issues we have discussed earlier in this section, and they are not good signs. We discuss this later in the feedback section of this chapter

Taken as a whole, then, we urge users of surveys to treat the response rate as if it were a question on the survey, and to interpret negatively any signs of low participation.

Data processing and analysis

In the paper and pencil version of the survey, completed documents are gathered together and typically, sent to a data processing house which keys in the numbers on each page. The Internet survey shines here because the keying has already been done by the employees. Whichever method is used, what is often a vast amount of "raw" data is produced which has no obvious meaning and must be processed. Once that is done, results can be graphically laid out by demographics such as larger organizational unit, and cross-referenced (for example, all management employees in Japan). As long as no data for groups of less than 8 persons are broken out (a typical cut-off which is communicated to employees), clients can and do ask for all sorts of information from this data pool.

Ranking: The secret of powerful analysis

One of the things which one learns in the business of morale is that some of the most powerful tools are the most simple. While it might seem obvious that a sophisticated statistical technique is required to bring the most valuable information out of the raw survey data, *nothing could be further from the truth*. Part of the reason for this is that morale data must be shared with many people at different levels in the organization. These people are not all trained in factor analysis, "t" tests, p<0.001, etc. They want straightforward answers to simple questions like "how is my group doing?" and they don't want an answer which starts with "there is one chance in 1000 that the null hypothesis is incorrect". We have always felt that our job as consultants was to bring the data to everyone in a simple yet powerful form, yet which was also underpinned by solid statistical foundations. Ranking gives us the chance to do that; it allows every group in the organization to be compared to any "whole", whether that whole is the total organization, or a subgroup. Let's look at some examples:

- *All UK versus organization-wide results*
- *North of England versus all UK*
- *Management in North of England versus management in all UK*
- *Management in UK versus management organization-wide*

In this way the comparison group against which an individual group is compared becomes an *internal "norm" or benchmark, and multiple norms are possible and indeed desirable.* Not only that, but these are norms which have huge value because they do not suffer from some of the problems we find in external norms, as we discuss below.

A simple ranking system

The Likert[2] 5-point scale is very common in most survey questionnaires; meaning a scale from 5 down to 1 with the two poles labeled with the most extreme options permitted. Survey respondents are directed at the beginning of the document to click or circle the number which most closely approximates their point of view.

An example would be a question like: "How do you like your job, the work you do?" This would typically be answered on a 5-point scale from "a great deal" to "not at all". Respondents have the options to say they like the job somewhat less than "a great deal" but more than "neutral", in which case they score a 4. On the negative side they can be somewhat negative without saying they don't like their job at all, by choosing a 2. Here is how the process works from there:

- On receiving the data, averaging the top two scores (a 5 or a 4) across all respondents, and for each individual question, gives you a "percentage favorable".
- A 3 score being neutral, averaging the 2 or 1 responses across all respondents for each individual question gives you a "percentage negative". (See Figure 2)
- Subtracting the "percentage negative" from the "percentage favorable" gives you the *net favorable response* for each question. In nearly all cases (unless your morale is in a sorry state indeed) this will be a positive number.
- Averaging these scores across all questions gives you a *single, understandable number* which can be compared to all groups in the organization. *You have just generated a "**morale index**".*

Before you go out and use this however, we need to discuss an important step which will let you use your index in more productive ways in your organization. The step is to decide the following: *on which questions in the survey would you say management (including first line supervisory roles such as "team leaders" etc.) has influence?*

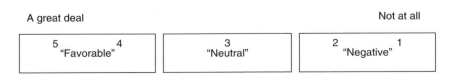

FIGURE 2 **Scoring for a simple ranking system**

By answering this question, you can adapt your morale index to a slightly reduced number of questions, but what you lose gives you a big added advantage:

- By leaving out questions on which individual members of management have little influence (such as how employees respond to items on the list of employee benefits, or how they respond to the credibility of "corporate" communications media, for example), what remains in your index are the questions on which they do have influence and for which the organization probably wishes to hold them accountable.
- By calculating the new morale index based only on those items, the organization can use the index to incentivize individual managers, based on the score. This is especially useful where morale is low in a particular area.

A more complex ranking system

For power users of surveys, there is another ranking system which creates it own morale index, and which has equal statistical validity. In order to understand the differences between the two ranking systems consider the following:

- Mary Smith's department scored a "25" on the morale index, which in her organization is calculated using only those survey questionnaire items on which management has influence. This was a score which was within ten percentage points of the overall organization average; so Mary was quite happy with the results.
- Mary was also pleased to see that her score had increased from "20" two years ago when the survey was last conducted.
- However the organization had additional information which gave them a concern: the overall organization had enjoyed a huge resurgence in morale, increasing 15 points since the last survey. Mary's department had increased only 5 points which meant that, relatively speaking, **Mary's department had slipped.**
- In other words, it is possible to do better in an absolute sense, but do worse in a relative sense. How does one reconcile these two aspects of the same organizational view? By using a second ranking system, and then making the decision as to how a particular group has performed on the survey, *based on both.*

The "relative" ranking system requires either a consultant who has the right program or some skilled help to create that programming; the latter path is the one which we took. Here is how the program works:

- The data are again examined for percentage favorable or negative. However, an additional calculation is carried out: the percentage favorable of an individual group is compared to the percentage favorable of the overall, organization-wide results,[*] *question by question.*
- If there is a positive ten-percentage point difference on the percentage favorable between the individual group and the whole, a score of +1 is assigned to that group, *for that question.* If the group is within ten percentage points of the whole, no score is assigned.
- The same action is carried out on the negative side: if a group scores less negative on a question by ten percentage points vs. the overall, it receives +1 point. Within ten percentage points of the overall, there is no score. If the group is ten percentage points more negative than the whole, the score is −1 (minus one point).
- The final score for a group is the sum total of all these "+1", "−1" and "zero scores". The overall organization is automatically scored zero, creating easy charting possibilities.
- Neutral scores (usually "3" on the Likert 5-point scale) are ignored.

Table 2 below shows this scoring system much more clearly:

TABLE 2   **Scoring for a more complex ranking system**

Condition	% Favorable Pole Score	% Negative Pole Score
+10% vs. overall	+1	−1
Within 10% of overall	Zero	Zero
10% vs overall	−1	+1

---

[*] Once this has been done for the overall organization, the group can be compared to another reference group, such as everyone in its same function, everyone in its same job level, everyone in its country, etc. Each ranking score then gives the organization a valuable reference point.

Example:

Question: "How would you rate your job, the kind of work you do?"
Overall organization: 65 percent Favorable, 15 percent Negative, 20 percent Neutral
Department X: 55 percent Favorable, 25 percent Negative, 20 percent Neutral
Department X score: $(-1) + (-1) = (-2)$
Reason for Score: Department is 10 percentage points less favorable (-1 score) and 10 percentage points more negative (-1 score) than the overall organization on this question.

Whichever system of ranking you use, you now have at your disposal a single quantitative measure with which you can:

- Compare the morale of groups to the overall and to each other.
- Compare the overall organization and its subgroups to themselves over time.
- Think much less about external norms because you have made your organization its own norm, and no organization in the world is exactly like you are.
- If you wish, set your own quantitative standards for how you want the organization to perform as far as morale is concerned, and not base that on what other organizations do.
- Easily communicate both the data and the methodology of analyzing it to your people.
- Create logically anchored incentives in the area of morale for your managers and/or teams, again easily communicated and understood.

If you use *both ranking systems* you can add one more benefit:

- Understand both the absolute moves and relative moves of morale in the organization; combining them provides the complete picture of morale and its movements over time for any group in the organization relative to any internal norm.

VIEWING THE MORALE INDEX: THE POWER OF A PICTURE

Very few things can grab the attention of management as images like those in the charts (Charts 1, 2 and 3) below. Taken from data

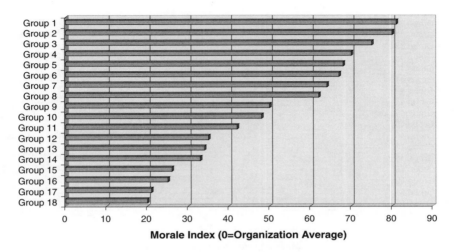

CHART 1   **Morale Index by Group, Typical Company Data:
Above Average Performers**

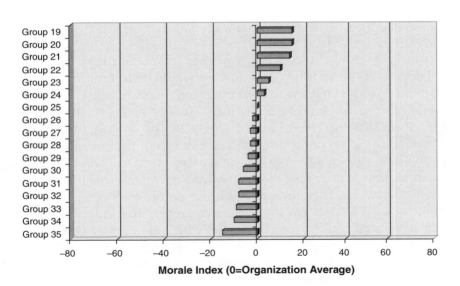

CHART 2   **Morale Index by Group, Typical Company Data:
Average Performance**

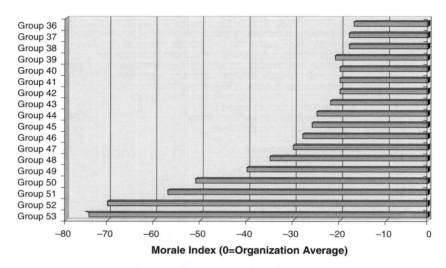

Morale Index (0=Organization Average)

CHART 3   **Morale Index by Group, Typical Company Data:
Below Average Performers**

generated across multiple client surveys, each bar is a key group within the organization. The *relative* morale index shown below is calculated according to the methodology which is detailed above, and for our clients usually involved data from at least 80 survey items, and sometimes 100+. It is therefore a very general view of how team members see things at work and how they feel about them.

Looking at this data on a spreadsheet would be interesting but it is nothing like the effect which computer graphics produce. With the *average for the whole organization normalized at zero*, deviations from that norm show up clearly and strikingly. By the time we reach Chart 3, and taking a ten point difference as our benchmark of significance between one group and another, we see that there truly are *huge internal differences in these (and most) organizations' morale levels.* This "first glance" view can therefore be a starting point, answering the question: "*how did we do?*" For some, the news is very bad indeed, but they will have a chance to see the details which lie behind this overall index and then to discover how the high performers in Chart 1 reached the levels which they did. Explaining how they came to be so very far below their own organizations' average will be a far more difficult task than comparing themselves to a less tangible "industry norm", especially when they see peer groups performing the same functions within the same internal culture but doing so much better than them.

Note that there is a "surge" in the positive data above certain points, in this case at +40 and again at +60. This frequently happens on both ends of the scale: the best performers are often "stand outs", as are the worst ones (see Chart 3 with "surges" below −30, −40 and −58).

EXTERNAL DATABASES ("NORMS"): TO USE OR NOT TO USE?

We suspect that our comments above about the confidentiality of Internet surveying techniques have already alienated about half of our consulting colleagues; what we say under this heading might alienate the other half! (Note: we wrote this book for the end user, not the consulting community, and believe we owe you all our experience and candid commentary based on this experience).

Norms are data collected from many organizations around the world, on many of the same questions which are used in typical employee surveys. It therefore makes sense that they would be a useful "benchmark" against which to compare one's organization, rather like comparing a particular bank to other banks' return on assets (ROA) or return on equity. On the face of it this seems reasonable. Except for one thing: ROA is a standard measurement, at least in large geographically bounded business areas like the EU or the United States.[*]

Employee opinions do not meet this standard of measurement:

- Many different survey methods are used in the many organizations whose data make up the norm: these can include Internet collection, paper and pencil collection, etc.
- Different instructions might have been used in each location, affecting the results.
- Different levels of confidentiality might have been promised in each location, regardless of the method of data collection used.
- Each "norm" has a different mix of industries, organization types (profit, non-profit, government, etc.). None has a "lock" on one

---

[*] We recognize that accounting standards are different between the United States and EU, although as we write, these may be coming together as the United States moves from Generally Accepted Accounting Principles (GAAP) to internationally accepted standards which are in effect in the EU.

industry since the survey business itself is significantly fragmented. If one is a technology company and one wants to be compared to other technology companies (a good idea unless you want to be compared to insurance companies, etc.) it is probably not going to be possible to find a place where many of your direct competitors' data is located.

The reasons above would have been sufficient for us to be skeptical about the use of external norms by themselves, had we not done some (unpublished) research on the subject which convinced us that we needed to stop them all together:

The utility industry norm comparison study

Every consultant in the business of conducting employee morale surveys wants to have external benchmarks to offer clients. These are major selling points, and a good looking benchmark often leads to a consulting project sale and beats out a competitor which does not have such an offering. For one of us who was intensively in this business for many years, the desire for such benchmarks was as strong as at any other firm.

Even some time ago, the use of benchmarks had become quite specialized, to the point where each industry (or if not an "industry", a service sector) could be pinpointed with its own benchmark. This meant that technology companies did not have to be compared to banks and police forces compared to factory workers. There is good reason for this: each attracts different types of people wanting different things. One industry (like the Post Office) might attract workers who are keen on job security, whereas technology assuredly does not, and has more of a focus on working for growth companies in exciting fields. In addition each industry wishes to compare itself as much as it can to its peers. This is done in exhaustive ways in the financial area of stock market analysis, where companies are compared by logical groupings like telecom, semiconductor, financial services, etc.

Of particular interest to us at one time was the US utility industry: with many thousands of workers engaged in generating, transmitting and selling energy (electricity and gas) to businesses and households across the country, the industry was and is a big user of morale research. These companies were stockholder owned, for the most part, rather like in post-deregulation Germany and the United Kingdom, for example.* With their interest in and demand for surveys, we had taken on something of a specialization in this field and had several utility clients throughout the United States. This in turn generated a database of responses which we formed into a "norm" for the industry, but it was not large enough for us and we wished to expand it.

We did this by doing something which was quite unusual: we asked companies for whom we had not done work to share their employee morale data with us, and about 20 did so. With a promise that their company data would never be shared with anyone else, except in the aggregate, we built trust and formed a larger database. However, what came with their data presented such a surprise to us: most, if not all, the companies had contracted with consultants to run their surveys, and most of these consultants had their own "utility norms". An opportunity presented itself to us which was rather like the "holy grail" of employee survey research: norms from different sources but the same time periods, targeting the same industry, could be compared with each other and with our own data. Such opportunities almost never present themselves in this fragmented industry which closely guards its competitive advantages such as data. Of course, fragmentation also meant that no one firm had a stranglehold on a majority, or even a large minority, of these types of companies.

After carefully matching questions and finding quite a few which were almost identical, we generated results which were shocking:

*There were sometimes differences of 10 **or even 20 percentage points** between the normative databases **on the same questions**.*

Assuming that 70 percent was the percentage favorable for one of these normative databases *on a particular question*, it might have been 10–20 percentage points (not percent) lower or higher for another. Our standard measure of a significant difference is 10 percentage points, which has been tested under many circumstances and more than meets tests of statistical significance in comparing one group with another and determining if they are statistically different. This meant that clients

---

* Even with extensive US deregulation, some cities like Austin, Texas and Los Angeles maintain a city-owned and operated utility company, typically offering much lower electric rates than investor-owned competition.

using this data would have very significantly different norms depending on their source of data. They would in turn not really know "how they are doing" against others, even in the same industry!

When these concerns were raised with potential and existing clients on this subject, we were often asked, *"How could this be? These were employees from companies in the same industry, responding in the same time period, on almost or completely identical questions. How can there be such a difference?"* Our reply was usually to point out the following:

- In a fragmented industry such as HR management consulting, no one firm has a "lock" on one industry's employee morale data. This means that data from different surveyed companies is distributed in a non-random way across different normative databases, and this can create large differences between the norms.
- Cultural differences (in turn created by leadership, history, etc.) between companies create differences even in the same industry.
- Subtle differences in questionnaire wording can cause responses to be different.
- Small differences in the way the questionnaire is distributed can cause differences on the responses, for example, what is said when questionnaires are delivered and how they are delivered (Internet distribution* or in group meetings).

Whatever the case though, the norms were different, and our confidence in them and the whole idea of external benchmarking was undermined. If such differences existed within normative databases *for one industry*, surely there must be bigger ones for an aggregate of all industries?

Shortly after this finding, we deleted our benchmarks from the computers, told clients why and explained that they would be much better off using internal ranking methods and past data for comparison purposes (where you "become your own norm"). Ironically we believed that *not having something* and explaining why, gave us a competitive advantage in an industry where having that very thing was seen as a huge advantage. The information about the utility industry norms was kept secret for the participants and was not published. Now that 20 years have passed, we feel more comfortable but realize that this will ruffle some feathers. For that reason we also present here

---

* Our example of the utility norms happened before Internet delivery was used.

some counter-arguments to our findings, which may give some comfort to those who make extensive use of external norms.

The Sirota comparison study

In their valuable and insightful book, David Sirota and his colleagues[3] mention a US-government normative study carried out in 2002 which generated a "public sector" norm of 100,000 federal employees as well as utilizing a pre-existing "private sector" norm generated from "large, primarily US corporations".

Sirota found that there were significant similarities between the data which his firm had collected between 1994–2003 (totaling over 3 million responses) and that of the government databases. The rank order correlation between the Sirota norm and the US-government private sector norm was 0.95 and between their norm and the government public sector norm 0.83. These are high correlations which present statistically very significant findings, and this is one of those rare cases where such comparisons are possible. Could it be that our data from the US utility industry represent an "outlyer", an unusual and non-representative finding, and that the Sirota data represent what is more common a case? *This is perfectly possible.* We still suggest further study is necessary in order to resolve the questions that have been raised.

One final comment on this subject comes from a researcher named Steve Bicknell, someone with extensive experience in this field (more than 100 global engagement studies), who shares our skepticism about comparison databases.[4] He comes to the conclusion that an employee-morale comparison of two car companies, for example, Bentley and Vauxhall (a GM brand in England) makes less sense than comparing companies which share similar cultures, levels of motivation, stages of development, communication styles, etc. We would add that this can be very hard to find, which is all the more reason to go with internal ranking as a core analysis tool.

FEEDBACK AND ACTION PLANNING

At the outset of conducting feedback and planning action which you need to take following an employee survey, it is imperative to make it clear that this information will not be used in some kind of "witch hunt". Few things can be worse than to associate the morale survey process with such a negative outcome. Since morale depends on how people are treated, if the very measurement process for morale is used to beat them, then in time, and not a long time, the process will break down and response rates will drop.

This does not mean that the survey and its follow-through is not used to make significant changes in the organization, it means that importance must be placed on *the way in which it is done*. The values of the organization must guide action here, in this very sensitive area. Typically the following steps are used in an effective feedback and action planning process:

Step 1: Senior management feedback

The process we tend to use at this stage is called *"Top Down, Bottom Up"*. The survey data lends itself to such a flow of information, which involves letting each "level" know the results in a downward cascading process and then asking each level to develop actions plans and make suggestions for change. At the local level many of these changes may be unique to the group which comes up with them, but the opportunity exists to bring all of these together in such a way that the best of them can be used organization-wide. It is not uncommon for top management in client companies to be almost literally pawing the ground for their employee morale data, as soon as it is available, and why not? Few topics are of such interest, especially to those who make this a top priority (those who don't usually aren't involved in this process, so this is a self-selected group). We have seen the management groups of well known companies sit still for 3 or more hours at a time to watch a PowerPoint show of their survey data, and even then to ask every conceivable question which will let them dig deeper into what they are seeing. One reason is very simple: these people are used to managing their business based on data, and *the HR aspect of the business rarely has such a large amount of data as when a survey is conducted*. Finally, top management can:

- come to grips with things which are often only anecdotal or come to their attention via the distorting filter of "the grapevine";
- numerically compare one group with another and with the whole, within the same building or worldwide;

- see changes over time, including downward trends which are an early warning or "leading indicator" for worse to come;
- look at whether changes they made as a result of the last survey have taken hold, or not (for example, a change of management in a location);
- even see how other companies might have responded to the same questions (with the caveats we have discussed above, of course); and
- clearly identify where new changes need to be made, in personnel, processes, etc.

It is hardly surprising, when one reads this list, that the level of interest is so high. Depending on the technology used, results might be available almost immediately following Internet polling. For those with an impatient streak (and that number seems to be increasing every year among management ranks) this is a welcome change from the "old days" of having to wait 4–6 weeks for paper and pencil surveys to be entered into computer systems and analyzed.

Depending on the experience of management, the top group might wish to have a special presentation of the data from their consultant (internal or external). This helps because there are usually issues which require expertise in interpretation, and mistakes can cause actions to be taken based on faulty interpretation or assumptions. We have worked with management groups which have had many years of experience in seeing survey results, but which insisted on our presence there to guide them through the latest results, for these reasons. Bear in mind too that with frequent changes in management ranks which some organizations experience, new members coming in from outside might be present who have little experience with survey data.

The most useful presentations dispense large amounts of data in a palatable form. Humor on the part of the presenter is essential, as are graphics. Executives will want to see the "big picture" (organization-wide results) and the biggest subgroups on one image, for comparison purposes. Our experience was that the ranking analysis, which we usually showed at the end, was the most anticipated part of the whole.

Step 2: Planning action, senior group

It is usually wise to wait a short while before jumping into taking action based on the survey results. The data need to sink in, and conclusions need to be drawn which may take a little time to form (immediate "gut reactions" may not be of the highest quality). Additionally, outlying subgroup data need to be examined, before one has enough of a clear picture to move ahead. We usually never did any action planning at the initial presentation, for this reason. Within a week or two the top group is usually reconvened, and the discussion moves into a structured process designed to answer any questions which have emerged since the initial presentation, discuss some underlying reasons for the results and start to delineate the steps which:

- can be communicated to all other levels as an "overall action plan" or "areas of focus" along with the data
- need to be taken organization-wide, such as a change to the benefit plan, a change in management at a fairly high level or a change in the content of organization-wide communications, etc.
- need to be delegated locally
- are aligned with strategic objectives of the organization, or *more importantly are aligned with morale improvement drivers such as those discussed later in this book.*

The fourth bullet above is extremely important: why focus on something which the survey indicated is poorly rated when that aspect or area is out of alignment with the strategy and direction of the organization? For example, if a unit is in the process of being disbanded, sold, reduced in scope, etc., a focus on its morale as a priority makes little sense. Or why focus on pay for performance at the individual level, if poorly rated, when one is moving to self-directed work teams with team-wide incentives?

Another aspect is the necessity of using absolute best practices to implement change. This can be best explained with a medical metaphor: the survey is an MRI, the reaction to it a form of "triage", or prioritization based on needs, urgency, etc. It makes no sense that one should use outdated, unproven or less effective methods of treatment, even if one has diagnosed and triaged the organization's needs very effectively, with the best available technology. *Bringing these two aspects together, best practices for both diagnosis and improving morale, unleashes the real power of survey follow-on.*

Any action plan at the top level should be limited, focused. It is a mistake to try and do too much, to promise too much. Two to three significant actions, diligently followed through, will get the attention and appreciation of the workforce. In any case, most issues are local, not organization-wide and so a limited and focused plan is appropriate. *The need for delegation (a major morale booster as we shall see) also necessitates limited action here.* Another issue here is the information flow: one very good reason for the top-level planning taking place before anything is communicated further into the organization is the fact that mid level management and all employees will be asking this question at their own presentation meetings, either in their heads or out in the open:

This is very interesting but what are you going to DO about it?

With an organization-wide focus in place and two or three steps outlined, there will be a chance for other levels of employees to see not only the data but a response which makes sense and *gives them a feeling they have been heard.* It is also a chance for top management to say: *"we've outlined some organization-wide steps but want you to look into your own data and take steps as needed, and we plan to ask what are YOU going to do about it?"*

Step 3: Mid level management feedback and action planning

Much like the senior group, most mid managers keenly await their results, while some await the moment with trepidation (if they had had poor results before, for example). For some organizations, presentations are made for each group by the consultants, while for others data are distributed in printed form or in electronic graphic form via the Internet. Perhaps a video presentation is made of the overall results, for all to see. Again, one wants the management team at all levels to know what the overall and group results look like before taking the next step: most organizations require that their mid managers down through team leader and supervisors meet with their teams to look at and discuss the data for their team.

Step 4: Organization-wide feedback and action planning

This fulfils a promise which, for all our clients, would have been made at the outset of a survey. This is true of any good survey process, whether conducted in-house or with outside resources. If a potential client said "no" to this step, we would respectfully refuse to work with them; such was the importance we placed on it. It was a commitment which we felt was so essential to the survey that not doing it made things worse than no survey being done at all.

As an employee relations exercise, this only enhances the benefits which have already accrued from conducting the survey and listening to the collective "voice" of the workforce. This is the time to surprise the doubters (of which there will be many) that there actually *will* be some feedback from this exercise and there *will* be some action taken. This is an investment in the future of morale in the organization which will have a high return on investment.

The ideal situation for feedback is at the small group or team level, with the leader or manager running the session. The exception to this is where the results are very bad, morale is very poor in this group and there is clearly no credibility for the team leader. In this case it is far better for an outside person, perhaps an expert in this area from HR or an outside consultant, to conduct the meeting. If the team leader in this situation does go ahead with the feedback it will be too tempting for that person to "brush over" the negative results or even completely leave them out (we have seen everything), or use defensive behaviors like blaming others.

When each level completes its feedback and action planning there will be everything from team-level goals to organization-wide ones. Ideally these are coordinated under an umbrella of change consisting of strategic needs, mission and values. The "best practices", ideas and actions which are planned from the team level on upward can be shared and may find their way into other areas well outside those which originated them.

Step 5: Consulting with managers on survey results

No matter how many times managers from the CEO to team leader have gone through the survey process, there will always be many questions which need to be answered, questions of interpretation of the data, about what to do in specific situations, etc. A fairly intensive level of "hand holding" should be built into the survey process from the outset in order to handle this, and, individuals need to be designated (and sometimes trained) to assist managers at all stages of the survey, but especially at this one. One of the most difficult things to do will be to help a manager deal with difficult data indicating poor morale in his or her area. This may or may not be the "fault" of that person but what-ever the case, it is now their responsibility. With "no witch hunt" as a guiding philosophy, the skilled practitioner will guide the manager through various levels of defensiveness, even to the point of grieving (this is not an overdramatization; receipt of negative survey results from a survey completed by one's team can be quiet traumatic).

The posture of denial is one which rears its head fairly often, and some managers will do anything to avoid responsibility and accept-ance of the results. For example, they will attack the survey methodol-ogy or the response rate or other aspects of the process, making it all the more important that that process be methodologically sound. In that way, *when the results appear, no factor other than the actual morale of the team creates the results which are found. Not a poor response rate, not a lack of confidentiality, nothing else than something internal to the work-ings of the team, something for which they are responsible.**

Having special software to rank results is a big advantage in this situation. To illustrate this, we will share with you an actual result from a survey we conducted:

At the end of the survey, the manager of an Emergency Room in an urban hospital was very upset because his results showed that the ER had the lowest morale across all departments in his hospital. He came to us and started to talk about the reasons why this had happened, but when he talked, all the factors which he mentioned were external to the actual workings of the ER team. He mentioned the bad neigh-borhood they all worked in, the violence surrounding the area, the number of victims of that violence coming into his ER every day and night. One of us who was listening to him waited until the moment was right and then produced a chart; the chart showed another, sister hospital's results (within the same system). The manager knew that this hospital served an equally awful environment, that an equal (or even greater) number of victims of violence were coming into its ER. But when he looked at the chart of survey data, he saw that, compared to the results from this second hospital, *the ER was the top scoring department for morale.* Better than intensive care, better than

---

* We are referring to a situation where a team's results are well below the average for the rest of the organization. In cases where morale is poor overall, responsibility for the results of a particular team might be traced back to cultural factors in the larger organization rather than the team itself.

pediatrics, better than everyone else. We asked him how this could be, and he was speechless, which is understandable. We then suggested respectfully that he take a trip to that hospital and find out what they were doing differently.

Our example demonstrates that methodologies which compare groups with the whole and with each other are powerful indeed, and can cut through the various forms of resistance which can occur in this field. Of course, in the case of the ER manager, no software can decide if the manager has what it takes to help his ER reach the level of morale of his peer hospital. That is another issue altogether.

RESURVEYING

Most organizations carry out a total "census" of the organization every year to eighteen months, although Internet polling makes things so much quicker and easier that that period is now shrinking. Intermittent sample surveys can now be easily carried out, which can achieve important goals:

- look at specific issues which may be an important focus (for example, if a large-scale change was made and a test of that change is necessary)
- carry out quick examinations of problem areas which have come to management's attention since the last organization-wide survey
- simply "take the pulse" overall to check trends, get early warning signals, etc.

If the organization has handled things well in the past, the survey can become a part of work life which is enjoyed, appreciated and actually adds to the very morale it is measuring. Our experience is that good managers look forward very much to getting their results, and eagerly consume them for indicators as to what to do better. Poor managers dread them and hope they will go away, and indeed their prayers are answered occasionally when a new CEO comes in with "his own ideas", which can include a negative attitude toward anything "touchy-feely". Surely, he never saw any of the data we are about to share with you.

CHAPTER 3

WHY MORALE IS SO IMPORTANT

INTRODUCTION

If there is one word which encapsulates the benefits which accrue from a high morale organization, it is this: **performance**. This refers to performance at the individual level and that of the organization as a whole. Evidence for morale correlating highly with, **and driving**, performance is strong and growing.

If you have competition such as most organizations in the private sector (although increasingly public sector organizations have competition), then high morale will increase your competitiveness. If you serve customers, your customers will be more satisfied when served by high morale employees; those customers will also be more likely to return to you. If profits are your goal, you will increase the likelihood of these. If you have a publicly traded stock,* even your earnings per share can correlate strongly with your morale level. If you are in the public sector and have a mission, like in the military or law enforcement, you will be much better at fulfilling that mission; indeed many in the military say that without good morale, missions become much more difficult or even impossible to achieve.

At the individual level, the high morale employee will experience less stress than the low morale one and as a result, less absenteeism and sick days; the high morale employee will be more engaged, willing to work harder, be more committed to the organization's goals than the low morale one, and will certainly be a stronger advocate for the organization with others such as customers, family and friends or potential employees.

---

* Earnings per share (EPS) of non-publicly traded stock might also behave this way, but we have seen no research which includes that category of security in this context.

Combining morale with organizational performance is one of the central focuses of the morale field of study, since consultants in this area are so often faced with the "so what?" question from some of the personalities we have detailed above, such as:

I like the general idea of high morale and it sounds like a good thing, but what does it really do for me?

An alternative and more negative view is often:

I'm in business to compete and make a profit; this stuff is a waste of time and wont change a thing.

Against this background and to counter these still widely held views, we will be presenting detailed evidence for the many *performance and effectiveness benefits* of the high morale organization in this chapter. Everything you will read on this topic is backed by solid data, in nearly all cases from multiple sources. To demonstrate just how powerful morale is, we will summarize many of the benefits here, then lay out the proof for these statements:

1. Morale provides a competitive edge in good times and bad

Writing a book about morale during turbulent times in financial markets is interesting for the way it focuses attention on what gives organizations an edge over others, even when times are difficult. Unfortunately morale is usually one of the last things on which an organization will focus in this situation: how many times have we heard the phrase, "We'll get to that when things improve".

The answer is simple: *"Why don't you use **this** to make them improve!?"*

Surviving a crisis (for the organization alone or for the society in general) is far easier when morale is high.[*] The team pulls together and works as one. Sacrifices are shared much more easily. Requests for them are greeted not with anger and resentment but understanding and willingness. Creative ideas for improvement are brought forward. "Employees" act more like "owners", not just people who will jump ship

---

[*] Churchill knew this and took advantage of it with his famous radio speeches to the British people during WWII.

when times get hard. High morale is therefore more than protective armour, although it does play that defensive role: it offers an *offensive* path through the crisis which those lacking it will not be able to follow.

It goes even further than this though: one does not need a melting stock market to face challenge, it is there every day. In this time when your service can suddenly be outsourced to Bangalore for one tenth your cost of providing it, when your products can be cloned and successfully launched in lucrative markets with no profit for your organization, and when everything like this moves so quickly, what edge do you have? You have **your people.** Bangalore can produce great looking Web pages but do they have your enthusiastic, committed staff which wakes up wanting to do its absolute best for your organization? Maybe they don't, and that is your edge.

2. High morale supports the implementation of organizational strategies

Imagine this conversation at a doctor's office:

> *Mr. Smith*: Doctor, I'd like to run the London Marathon.
> *Doctor*: OK, let's do some tests and see what shape you're in.
> *Two hours later, Doctor*: Mr. Smith, I don't think you can safely run around more than one city block, in fact I would advise against you even attempting that.

In other words: it's not your plans that are important; its whether you can *implement* them. Translation into the organizational world: a good strategy is a fine thing, but it is useless unless you can make it happen. Making it happen depends to a large degree *on your people,* and therein lies the power of morale. Of course the problem is that this is so far from what is taught at business schools in MBA and other programs, which are often *strategy* and *finance* oriented. Don't just take our word for it, even those who teach there agree.[1] We're here to help try and fill that gap.

3. The morale process (measurement-implementation) gives employees a voice

It sounds like a circular argument, but it is true: simply measuring morale and feeding back the results, *when carried out correctly*, improves morale. Over and over again, employees have thanked us for being in their organization, collecting their opinions and letting them know how they and their colleagues feel as a group. As we have mentioned above, there is usually intense interest in these results. In organizations where information has been closely controlled (and information is a major control lever, as we shall see), the process of opening things up is liberating: the voice of the "lowest"* level person can be heard. In organizational terms, it is the closest to democracy that most can come, in environments not always known for such high-minded concepts!

4. High morale helps organizations *attract* and *retain* talented people

Walking into a Starbucks Café one day, one of us was greeted by a large sign designed to recruit new *baristas* who would dispense coffee cheerfully and efficiently. The sign called out in large lettering: *One of the Top 100 Places to Work!!* It was referring to the annual survey of US companies conducted by *Fortune Magazine*, in which employees are asked a series of morale-measuring questions about their organization, their job, benefits and so on. We asked one of the baristas there if in fact this was true for her, in this particular location, (knowing that even high average scores for the whole company can hide negatives on one tail of the bell curve, although we didn't bias her response with that little statistical fact); she replied immediately that indeed it was a great place to work, with its flexible shifts and great benefits (Starbucks was and still is well known for giving full benefits for employees who work even half time, something very unusual for the United States; many single mothers work there for that very reason.)

Needless to say (but we will say it anyway), organizations selected by *Fortune* and the UK equivalent Sunday Times Best Places to Work, trumpet their appearance on such lists in recruitment advertising, not just at the point of sale like the Starbucks example, but also in newspaper and online ads. They are eager to let the world know how good it is to work for them, and the fact that it is their own employees who have said so, is even better.

---

* We use the word "lowest" in quotes because of the delightful practice some organizations have in inverting the organizational chart, making the CEO "lower" than all other employees. We will cover this issue later.

Of particular importance here is not just the fact that the high morale organization can attract people in general, but especially *talented people*; often this level of quality individual, having more choice than most by virtue of their talent, will refuse to work somewhere which has a bad reputation for employee relations, morale, etc.

For the same reasons that make a person want to work there, retention is also significantly affected by high morale. People will stay in organizations which treat them well; the costs avoided by not having to replace them are enormous.

5. High morale makes the workplace easier to manage and increases productivity

Stripped of the dramas created by negative morale situations and the challenges of dealing with people who like to perpetuate them (from individuals with no management responsibility to managers themselves), the high morale workplace becomes less fearful, stressful and more "fun". Management time can be focused on things which make the organization more productive, not just "putting out fires" related to personnel, or replacing the people who have left (see above). For the average employee, the energy which went into simply surviving the day is channeled to work instead.

In a high morale environment, people can't wait to get to work and be productive. In a low morale environment, people can't wait to leave work: at 5 p.m. sharp, the place empties out. These are the environments which invented and perpetuate the phrase TGIF (Thank God It's Friday). One can be sure that Google employees don't chant TGIF every week or empty the parking lots at 5.10 p.m. every day. It doesn't take much imagination to see that the time spent between arrival and departure is quite different, from a productivity perspective, in the high morale workplace.

6. High morale reduces workplace accidents, absenteeism, workplace stress, improves employee health and reduces sick days taken

Plenty of evidence exists for all of these claims; in fact the evidence is so overwhelming that it is hard to imagine why organizations do not implement practices which would lead to a maximum level of morale, even if only to gain just these advantages; and yet many do not.

7. High morale, driven by culture, also supports that culture

As we mentioned when discussing our model of morale, we believe the best definition of "culture" as it refers to the organizational environment is, "the way we do things around here".[2,3] It is simple and exactly to the point. Deal and Kennedy's groundbreaking book, *Corporate Cultures*, opened the subject of culture up for the organizational world and turbocharged the development of a whole industry of consultants in the field, one of us among them! Born of some frustration with the then-current organizational theories, the book attempted to bring to light some mysterious state which seemed to control the way organizations functioned, whether they succeeded or failed. For example, it was clear that strategy alone was not sufficient to explain everything, nor was organizational structure; but what was the secret ingredient which made things work, or not as the case may be? Culture was the perfect prism through which one could view the organization in a new way. Every organization has one, however weak or unintentional; and from that culture comes morale and ultimately, performance. Deal and Kennedy point out that it is culture which ties people together with a sense of purpose. As they say, perfecting this aspect of organizational life is one of the reasons for Japanese success in the industrial world.[4]

Morale fits into the equation with culture in a two-way relationship:

Culture can create the basis for high morale
Morale can support and sustain the stated and desired culture

Consider the phrase *"we put people first"*. Many organizations like to say this; they put it in their employee handbook, tell it to potential recruits and stress it in annual reports. As such it is what the Germans call a *Leitbild* ("guiding picture"), which certainly has the potential to guide how morale develops within the organization. If we say this with slight reservation, it is because not all "guiding pictures" make it past the picture stage. No doubt, though, that intentions are good when this phrase is first communicated, and having it "out there" is certainly a sign from top management that *this is what we are, this is what we believe, this is how we want our workplace to be*. If it is truly allowed to guide the "way we do things around here", it can and will ensure a high morale workplace.

In the reverse direction, once high morale is established, it perpetuates the cultural principles, makes the picture "real".

8. High morale helps organizations work better with unions

We take no position for or against unions, having worked in many unionized factories, mines, airlines, electric utility companies, etc. We also confess to having a sense of the history of unions, which makes for a compassionate feeling for why they developed in the first place. Its hard to live and work for years in Manchester, United Kingdom, birthplace of the industrial revolution, and while there to work in the area of industrial psychology, and not have that sense. Union employees want a high morale environment as much as anyone else, and they enthusiastically take part in processes to measure and improve morale. Unions and high morale absolutely can and do coexist.

Having said that, can organizations help themselves with unions simply by creating a high morale environment? The answer is definitely, yes. Union demands often increase where companies have let things slip with their workforce in some way, whether in pay equity, working conditions, safety or other factors. It makes sense if a company preempts this by improving the work environment to the level where union demands would not be triggered, and the working relationship between trade unions and management is likely to be enhanced. It also happens that improving this environment increases morale, benefiting the organization as a whole, especially its performance. This in turn can pay for any costs associated with improving morale, if any: frequently, actual costs of such improvement are zero.

9. High morale organizations in the for-profit world have better financial performance than low morale ones

Some people fresh from high intensity MBA programs, or still in them, might be only partially convinced of the importance of morale at this stage, given our emphasis so far on HR outcomes as a result of high morale. So we have something especially for them: there is strong evidence from multiple and highly credible sources that *morale is positively correlated with higher stock prices, higher earnings per share, and even 5-year survival following an IPO.*

10. High morale organizations can have higher customer satisfaction than low morale ones

In our case study of a successful and high morale European organization (Chapter 4), we present a detailed account of this company's experience of merging customer satisfaction with employee morale data. The results were astounding, showing a connection which was even more powerful than we had predicted. This company is not alone in its findings: a great deal of research shows the morale-customer satisfaction connection, and demonstrates causal connections between the two, as we shall see.

11. Morale is a leading indicator and allows organizations to prevent potential negative situations

Something which we have observed on a regular basis is that morale can be a *leading indicator*. How can we say this? Because there are two areas, one internal to the organization, one external, in which we have made the following observations:

- Morale scores tell you what is happening now, much of which you might not have known. Looking deeper into the data, and picking out specific "power" questions (more on that later), you will see what is deteriorating and what is improving, in your organization. By examining trends based on previous data you have collected, you can have a sense of how the future will play out if you take no action. This is especially true when a poorly performing manager is having a negative effect on employee morale; indeed, this analysis often prompts clients to take action before things get worse.
- As you will see from our case study, a client which took the time and expense to dig deeper than any other we have met, discovered that employee morale, when measured two years ahead of customer satisfaction, could actually predict the latter with some accuracy. This was not true in the other direction. This so-called time-series analysis demonstrated that, at least in the client we surveyed, the morale data could act as a leading indicator of customer satisfaction.

12. The morale process is one of the most democratic activities in which an organization can participate.

One of the main reasons why the process of measuring, feeding back results and acting on morale issues in the organization is so powerful is the fact that there is nothing quite like giving every single person who works there the chance to say exactly what they feel, knowing that top management will look at every piece of data and every written word. Given the power structure in the organization, the ability of "higher ups" to use rewards such as pay and promotions and to actually take away one's livelihood if they should so choose, the motivation to be as honest about the way things are is significantly reduced, under normal circumstances.

The employee survey gives even the most humbly positioned person the right to, figuratively, travel across the country if necessary (or even round the world), take the lift to the top floor or walk to the corner office and speak their mind. Done right, this can be achieved with complete confidentiality, and with no negative side effects for that person. Where else in organizational life can one say this? When else can one say that the voice of the employees can have a "boss from hell" sacked? Can change company policies about anything from smoking to parking to executive dining rooms, to promotional practices, to rampant favoritism, to office layout or factory lighting or heating, to entire pay programs? Employees appreciate this, they say so in the surveys themselves, they say almost invariably that they have an intense interest in the "results of this survey". As a method of democratizing the workplace, few activities even come close to the morale measurement and improvement process.

13. High morale at the individual level is connected to job performance by that person, and is *as good a predictor of that performance as other, well tested measures*

Long before researchers began to look at the effects of group morale on performance, they had undertaken the task of connecting the two at the individual level. Not only is there significant connection, but multiple studies now demonstrate that there are few activities one can undertake better than knowing a person's individual level of morale, in order to predict how they will perform on the job.

Actually high morale does even more than all the above, as we shall see; and the evidence which supports it is compelling. We can summarize by saying that creating and sustaining high morale as a goal is a more than worthwhile effort in any organization, with a *huge return on investment*.

WHY MORALE IS SO IMPORTANT 1: GROUP MORALE, FINANCIAL PERFORMANCE AND ORGANIZATION EFFECTIVENESS

We have presented a lot of statements about what morale can do for the organization without giving you the proof; we will now fill that gap Many studies have been done to connect morale and performance, and some of the best are presented here. We will look first at those studies which link *whole organizations or business units* to performance outcomes, and then examine the connection between *individual* morale and performance. As a first step though we need to look briefly at criteria for judging organizational performance and the history behind this, since these criteria are critical to our discussion of the morale connection.

Warning! The tone of writing shifts here for a short while, by necessity. Perhaps up to this stage you feel that you have been skiing downhill through glorious landscape as you read this book, at least we hope you feel that way! However, in order to convince you that morale and performance are strongly connected, we need to enter the world of research in some depth, so that you are not just depending on our opinions. This may feel like your ski run has suddenly hit grass, and we apologize for this. We will have you back on the snow as soon as possible!

Performance measures

In a paper whose research findings we will discuss later in this chapter, James R. Evans and Eric P. Jack[5] examine and summarize quality measurement criteria in a succinct way. As the authors point out, until Kaplan and Norton's introduction of the Balanced Scorecard in 1992[6] and later in book form in 1996,[7] most organizational performance measures were both limited and limiting, and based on simple accounting criteria. They were limiting due to the impossibility to shoehorn the measurement of complex strategic plans' outcomes into such simple criteria. Kaplan and Norton's criteria expanded these criteria into a more "balanced" version consisting of four areas:

- Financial: this takes shareholders' interests into account and focuses on such factors as profits, ROI, share price and total shareholder return, etc.
- Internal: these factors include quality and productivity measures.
- Customer: the focus here is customer satisfaction and market share and the drivers of that such as quality of customer service.
- Innovation and learning: this includes the people side of the organization, what we would call employee morale, the skills of the workforce, etc.

As the authors say, there is little significant difference between the Balanced Scorecard approach and the measurement factors which are included in national and pan-national quality awards programs such as the (US) Malcolm Baldrige National Quality Award for Performance Excellence and the EFQM Excellence Award in Europe. All include human resource, customer, financial/market and organizational effectiveness factors: essentially all the Baldrige and the EFQM criteria can be appropriately slotted into the Balanced Scorecard focus areas, and vice versa.

Of particular interest, they point out the importance of time-related perspectives in the measurement process:

> The anecdotal evidence suggests that a good balanced scorecard contains both leading and lagging measures and indicators. Lagging measures (outcomes) tell what has happened; leading measures (performance drivers) predict what will happen. For example, customer survey results about recent transactions might be a leading indicator of customer retention (a lagging indicator); employee satisfaction might be a leading indicator for turnover, and so on.[8]

The authors' article is an examination of the linkages between these various factors, which are interesting and complex, and for which there is increasing empirical evidence. The reason for this complexity is that the *same factor can be both an input (leading indicator) and an output (lagging indicator)*. An example of this would be customer satisfaction: in its leading indicator role it would "drive" profits; in its lagging indicator role, it would be "driven by" high employee morale.

In the context of our examination of morale and performance, then, it is clear that morale (although sometimes under a different name) is recently always considered in measures of quality and organizational effectiveness. The quality movement, the national and international quality awards programs have all raised morale's profile as a result. Less frequent is the focus on morale's effect on lagging indicator performance measures of financial performance, although this is increasing. Our account of the morale-performance connection will therefore take these multifaceted effects into consideration in our examination of some of the best and largest-scale available research. The issue of scale is critical here: while some academic research in this area can be extremely well designed and executed, it does not compare to that conducted by international consulting groups in terms of the numbers of employee responses measured. We will therefore make use of both corporate and academic research to tap the huge scope of the former and the methodological strength of the latter.

The Gallup research

Gallup is a large international opinion polling and consulting organization best known for its political polls. It also works worldwide with employee opinions which it measures in many locations. Having a massive employee opinion database lends credibility to any morale-performance data which is presented, which is why we begin here. According to its recently published web material, Gallup has no less than *5.4 million employees in its database, with data collected in 137 countries and 45 languages.*[9] * Like other consultants in this area, they focus less on morale in general than on the subset we examined in the first chapter of this book, *employee engagement*. Gallup suggests that only 29 percent of the average US organization's employees can be defined as "engaged", as measured by its 12-item questionnaire on the subject. However, according to Gallup, these employees are *more productive, produce more profits, are more oriented toward the customer, and are more likely to stay with the organization.*

---

* Of the 5.4 million employee opinion responses in its overall database, Gallup has 3 million responses since 1997 to its special "Q12" question series of 12 questions on employee engagement, from which it generated this analysis.

These are powerful statements coming from analysis of such a large database, and as Gallup suggests, they "put to rest" questions as to whether there is a connection between engagement (which we define as a subset or result of morale) and performance on the job. If that is not enough, the research goes further to establish firm correlations between engagement and company financial performance. The following chart (Chart 4) shows the connection between earnings-per-share (EPS) and engagement: in the highest performing companies in their database, ranked by EPS (those in the top quartile of EPS performance), engagement levels are far higher (4.1: 1 ratio of engaged to disengaged) than in the bottom half of those EPS ranked companies (0.96: 1 ratio engaged to disengaged).

Looked at in terms of EPS growth over time, similar results are found. When this is done, Gallup found that the top quartile (for employee engagement) companies in its database had much higher EPS growth in two time periods: 2001–03 and 2004–05: 2.4 percent

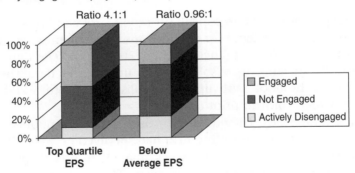

Disengaged Employees Depress Performance

A comparison of publicly traded companies in which Gallup has surveyed employee engagement, sorted into two groups: top 25% of EPS performance and lower 50% of EPS performance. The comparison shows top EPS performers have a ratio of 4.1:1 engaged employees to actively disengaged employees. Below average EPS performers have far less actively engaged employees (0.96:1)

Data and chart reproduced with permission of the Gallup Organization and BAI Banking Strategies*

CHART 4   **Ratio of engaged to disengaged employees among top quartile EPS and bottom two quartiles ("below average") EPS of Gallup Employee Engagement Database**

*Please see www.bai.org for more on this organization and its publicly available articles.

versus −2.9 percent for the first time period and 18 percent versus only 3.1 percent for the second (see Chart 5).

**Engaged Employees Drive Higher Performance:
EPS Growth Over Time Shown for each of Two
Employee Engagement Levels**

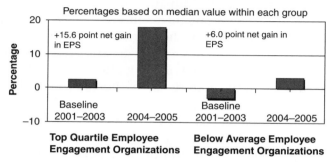

Data and chart reproduced with permission of the Gallup Organization and BAI Banking Strategies

CHART 5   **Comparison of top quartile (employee engagement) and bottom two quartiles (employee engagement) groups by EPS Growth, 2001–03 and 2004–05.**

The Sirota research

Industrial psychologist and consultant David Sirota and his colleagues provided valuable evidence for connections between employee morale and organization performance in their 2005 book *The Enthusiastic Employee*.[10] The authors also followed up on the data they had presented in the book with updates published later in a 2005 press release,[11] which confirm prior results.

For the 2002 study, they used their own data from publicly traded companies that their consulting firm had surveyed between 2000 and 2001, combined with the down stock market (minus 19 percent) of 2002 as their measure of performance. The authors divided the companies' *overall morale scores* (which they call "employee satisfaction") into three categories:

- High morale: 75% + favorable employee satisfaction scores
- Medium morale: 74% to 60% favorable scores
- Low morale: Less than 60% favorable scores

They did not say how many companies were involved with this original study until the updated version in 2005 which indicates that they had been tracking 750,000 employees from some 24 companies over the previous 5-year period.

When the stock market performance of the 2002 sample companies were compared *to their industry peers*, the results were striking: "high morale" companies actually had an increase in stock price during the calendar year, while low morale ones dropped more than the market. For the high morale group, the difference in stock price compared to their peers in 2002 was +20 percent, and for the low morale group, –5 percent. Sirota and his colleagues point out that when this analysis was extended to other performance measures such as return on assets and return on investment, the results were similar.

In the 2005 update, data for 2004 and 2005 were used and confirmed the direction of the earlier results, but with much more extreme differences between high and low morale organizations: those with high morale had more than double the stock market gains than those with medium or low morale, *compared to their peers*.

Table 3 summarizes this data; note that the table column titled "Ratio of Gains in Stock Performance" refers to the difference in percentage terms between the high morale group and its industry peers or the medium/low morale group and its peers. These differences are striking, to say the least.

The authors conclude that this evidence is compelling for a relationship between these variables, but the direction of the connection is left up in the air, due to the impossibility of deducing causality from concurrent correlation studies. As we will see later, however, this issue has been covered by other researchers, in some depth. These other studies essentially confirm the flow from morale to performance but with feedback loops back to morale.

Fortune magazine's "100 best companies to work for" and stock performance

The US business magazine *Fortune*, like the *Sunday Times* in the United Kingdom, produces a yearly feature on the 100 best places to work in its home country. They do this by having an outside

TABLE 3   Sirota analysis of morale relationship to financial performance, 2004–05

Morale level of company	Description	2005 Stock Gains	Ratio of Gains in Stock performance
High morale	> than 70% average overall employee satisfaction	+19.44%	+240%
Industry average	Other companies in same industries	+8.09%	
Medium and low morale	< than 70% average overall employee satisfaction	+10.13%	−188%
Industry average	Other companies in same industries	+19.08%	

Morale level of company	Description	2004 Stock Gains	Ratio of Gains in Stock performance
High morale	> than 70% average overall employee satisfaction	+16.31%	+267%
Industry average	Other companies in same industries	+6.1%	
Medium and low morale	< than 70% average overall employee satisfaction	+11.66%	−170%
Industry average	Other companies in same industries	+19.81%	

Source: Sirota Survey Intelligence, 2005. Reproduced with permission.

Institute[*] survey many companies' employees and also by conducting what they call a "Culture Audit" of management practices. As the co-founder of the Institute which gathers this data for *Fortune*, Robert Levering, pointed out in an interview published on a UK website,[12] when these data were correlated with stock market performance by a Wall Street firm, the results were astounding: the *Fortune Best Places to Work For companies outperformed the general market by almost 5:1.* Levering points out that a similar finding has been made with data collected in Britain and Brazil.

Of course, care should always be taken to make this apparent connection one of causality (morale>stock price): perhaps the stock

---

[*] Fortune works with the *Great Place to Work Institute* of San Francisco. In 2009 this survey involved 81,000 employees from 353 companies responding to a 57-item questionnaire.

prices going up drove employee stock options higher and made everyone happy, landing those companies on the list? Perhaps just being named in Fortune's *"Best Places to Work For"* list lead investors to place their money in as many of the 100 companies as they could (not all are tradable), much like the list were a mutual fund? This would make morale a "self-fulfilling prophesy", since investors would make this investment on the reasonable assumption that having high morale would indeed drive performance, along with the favorable publicity generated by the magazine article. So to suggest at this point that the high morale which is implied in the winners on this list *drives stock performance*, would be premature without a more sophisticated time-based analysis of the data. That type of analysis, of other performance factors, will be forthcoming in several of the studies below.

The Hay Group research

Hay Group is large international human resources consultant which has an active research arm for which one of us used to work. This arm of Hay collects over *one million employee responses a year* in survey or focus group form. Hay is best known for its work in compensation and job evaluation, or measuring the "size and scope" of a job, while the research arm generates significant amounts of data on employee morale and engagement. A team of their compensation experts wrote a book[13] which gives some interesting insight not only into rewards and their effect inside the organization (including on morale), but also into morale and performance. In a press release, Hay summarizes this proprietary research as follows:

> highly engaged employees can improve business performance by up to 30 per cent and ... fully engaged employees are 2.5 times more likely to exceed performance expectations than their "disengaged" colleagues[14]

The authors specify that this engagement level is something which is part of the "work climate* ... created by the manager", a finding with

---

* Hay defines "climate" here as a local level of what we would call morale, driven by management behaviors. In meteorological terms this might be referred to as a "micro-climate" which can be affected even by very small differences in terrain, etc. This compares to how Hay sees "culture", which is based on larger scale, group characteristics.

which we would strongly agree. We would also note here that their summary refers to both group ("business") performance and that of the individual being impacted by the engagement level.

The Maister research

David Maister is a management consultant specializing in professional service firms such as advertising agencies, law firms, etc., and it is with these firms that he has studied the connections between morale and performance quite extensively. In a valuable study conducted with a large multinational advertising and media company,[15] he was able to demonstrate effectively not only the connections between morale and financial performance but also show causality between these variables.

To do this, Maister surveyed 5500 employees in 139 offices of the company located in 15 countries. The questionnaire consisted of some 74 items which were condensed into 9 factors using the statistical technique of factor analysis.

Financial data were collected for many of the offices using a combination of:

- Two-year percentage growth in revenues
- Two-year percentage growth in profit
- Profit margin
- Profit per employee[16]

All four measures were averaged and weighted equally.

At this point Maister had conducted a classic study which allowed for correlations of variables having to do with employee morale with those which, theoretically, are "caused" by different morale levels. His first step was to show those correlations, and they were strong: by taking the 20 percent financially best performing offices, he demonstrated that they performed better on nearly all the employee "satisfaction" survey questions, significantly so on 69 of the 74. Of particular interest, the top 20 percent scored higher on 7 key items which had to do with the perception of managers' behavior (listening, being good coaches, being trustworthy, having good communication, etc.). This is extremely familiar to us because it ties in with our earlier comment that management is the key to high morale. Maister points out that it is management behavior, not corporate policies, which stand out in this way.

When Maister looked at the overall performance of *all offices* on which he had financial data, he found that fully 85 percent of employee survey items correlated positively with financial performance. Interestingly, the factor (grouping of employee survey questions) which statistically "explained" fully one quarter of financial performance was Quality and Client Relationships. These were questions which drilled down deeply into the way employees saw clients being treated, the quality of work provided, the emphasis on quality in the firm, the extent to which clients were well informed, etc. Some readers will recognize these as elements of what is called "Climate for Service", which we will cover in more depth in this chapter in the section "Why Morale is So Important 3: Morale and Customer Satisfaction".

Correlation not being the cause, however, Maister could not test his theory of employee "satisfaction" *causing* improvements in financial performance without going further, which he did using the sophisticated statistical technique of *structured equation modeling* (SEM), and based on his strong background in statistics. The SEM analysis produced what Maister describes as "extraordinary" results and data consistent with the conclusion that certain factors *caused* the financial performance of the successful offices to be that way. Included in these findings were the following:

- The quality and client relationships factor *was shown to have a causative relationship to financial performance*
- A one-point improvement,[*] such as going from a "Somewhat Agree" response to a "Agree" response on survey questions in the quality and client relationships factor *was associated with a doubling of financial performance* in an office.
- Two factors, employee satisfaction (general questions in areas we would define as "overall morale") and "High Standards" (questions on the quality of professionals in the office, expectations for high levels of performance, putting client needs above those of the office, etc.) *were shown to have a causative relationship to quality and client relationships.*
- Because of this causal chain from employees' quality issues to financial performance, it was possible to demonstrate again that a one-point shift on the Employee Satisfaction factor *was associated with more than a 40 percent improvement in office profit.*

---

[*] In this case this would be a one-point movement on a 6-point scale, or a 16 percent change on the measurement scale.

Other performance research: High performance management practices, quality award criteria (Baldrige, EFQM) and total quality management

The Pfeffer book

In his groundbreaking book entitled *The Human Equation*,[17] Jeffrey Pfeffer provides one of the most comprehensive views of the connection between people-centred management practices and organizational performance. While not specifically about morale (interestingly, the word "morale" does not appear in the book's index although frequent references are made to morale elements such as trust, commitment, etc.), the book is a treasure trove of data on the "people connection": the value of investing in people as measured by internal and external* performance outcomes.

Speaking in general terms of the value of this investment, Pfeffer notes that a return of 30–50 percent is possible through the implementation of what he calls "high performance management practices". These include elements which we have discussed and will also cover in more detail as we discuss how to build the high morale organization:

- Control, in terms of a say in how work is carried out; this is a motivator which leads people to work harder
- Allowing for smarter working by building skills and allowing/encouraging people to use them on the job
- Decentralization and de-layering of the organization, placing responsibility in the hands of people at lower levels

Pfeffer's examples of relevant research into high performance management practices (HPMP) demonstrate that the effects are clear:

- Studies showing stock market value per employee greater by 14% for those companies implementing HPMP
- Research showing that HPMP is correlated with much greater survival 5 years after initial public offerings of stock (IPOs)

---

* We use "internal" here to refer to factors such as productivity, absenteeism, scrap percentages, etc. "External" refers to financial performance, stock market value, etc.

- Demonstrations of huge gains in productivity (for example defect rates lower by almost 50%) when elements of HPMP ("flexible production") were implemented in an automobile manufacturing environment
- Steel industry implementation of HPMP driving 34% fewer labour hours per ton of steel and a 63% improved scrap rate.[18]

Pfeffer points out that of 131 studies carried out on the connection between HPMP and performance between 1961 and 1991, fully 75 percent reported significant economic improvement as a result.[19, 20]

Baldrige award criteria and performance

In a valuable addition of new data to the field, two authors whose work we quoted earlier, James R. Evans and Eric P. Jack, wrote a 2003 *Quality Management Journal* article[21] about research which set out to test 20 hypotheses related to the relationship between various performance "input" and "output" measures, including employee "satisfaction". The hypotheses drew from the Baldrige criteria which we discussed, and used a database based on a survey of 307 small, medium and large companies in all 50 US states across many industries. Using an advanced statistical technique called canonical correlation, they were able to test the hypothesized linkages in a powerful and interesting way. It should be noted that their definition of employee satisfaction is somewhat different than ours, in that it is derived not from employee opinions but from a "downstream"* combination of absenteeism rates, employee grievances and turnover.

Among the 20 hypotheses which they tested, those directly related to employee satisfaction were that it would be directly linked to:

- Process performance
- Service quality
- Product quality
- Market performance

---

* "Downstream" is used here in the same sense as in the oil business: something which is derived from an earlier product. In this case grievances, turnover and absenteeism are assumed to derive from the earlier psychological states which make up employee satisfaction.

In turn, these factors were projected to be linked through the chain of "output" variables up to, and including, financial performance, *thereby giving employee satisfaction at least an indirect connection to the financial end results of the organization.*

The results were a resounding confirmation of the Baldrige (and EFQM) models. The authors conclude that:

■ The factors which are part of the Baldrige model, including those management practices that have to do with employee well-being and motivation, are correlated strongly with each other and with other practices like the design of work systems.
■ Secondly, the internal factors on which the Baldrige/EFQM models focus are correlated with external performance measures such as market share, customer satisfaction and financial performance.

Taken together, these findings confirm the importance of the Baldrige/EFQM model and its focus on the input variables as drivers of performance. Much like the Pfeffer data, these crucial performance drivers center on the high performance management practices with which we have become familiar in this chapter.

The authors conclude that further research is needed, using even more sophisticated statistical modeling such as SEM, to reconfirm the causal relationships between these variables to which their research points.

Total Quality Management (TQM), employee involvement and performance

In another study carried out in a broad sample of manufacturing companies in Australia and New Zealand,[22] TQM practices were measured against organizational performance. Since TQM includes significant employee-oriented processes designed to raise morale, and since the study above demonstrates the positive effect on morale of such actions, these findings are very relevant for our review. The authors found that for a typical company in the database, there was significantly more likelihood of better performance in the "output" areas of operational performance, general business performance and customer satisfaction with TQM than without.

Employee morale/satisfaction and performance in the public sector: A school study

Most of our quoted research so far has been from the private or business sector, but the morale-performance connection is by no means limited to that. The public sector functions of education, law enforcement, military, public health care systems and others all benefit from it. While the public sector can present challenges as far as performance factors are concerned, well-designed studies like the one we will now examine find ways to measure this factor successfully. The study we are referring to was conducted in *298 schools and involved 13,808 teachers and 24,874 students at the high school level.*[23]

Three areas were measured to generate satisfaction and performance data:

- *Teacher satisfaction and other attitude measures* were measured using questionnaire items, selected from previously published inventories of such questions, and focused on typical morale elements such as
  - General attitudes toward their school, co-workers, supervision, pay, administration, facilities and parental support.
  - Commitment items related to whether they planned to continue working at the school, etc.
  - Adjustment items related to a sense of confidence in the school and their job, a sense of belonging, etc.
  - A stress scale involving items related to workload and related issues.
- *School performance* was measured both from the students' emotional perspective in terms of their satisfaction as well as what the author called "student productivity": broad factors of academic achievement, student behavior, teacher turnover and administrative performance which were themselves broken down into subfactors.[24]
- *School characteristics* were included in the study as well: how many non-minority students were at the school, governance such as public or private, and age of school buildings.

The findings of the study were clear: *there was a strong correlation between teacher satisfaction (what we would call morale) and the performance of the school.* Interestingly, this held even when characteristics of the school (the items listed above) were controlled through regression analysis. The authors were able to state that schools which had satisfied teachers were more effective than those which did not. Causality was not controlled through any special statistical or other measurement techniques, and the authors could not say unequivocally that the relationship between morale and performance did not move in both directions; they concluded (as we did in our Introduction) that it probably did.

Moving toward causality: factoring in the time element in morale > performance research

Another extensive study of the effects of HPMP or high performance management practices (including TQM and employee involvement) was carried out by management professor Dr. Edward Lawler and his colleagues in 1998.[25] Taking *Fortune* 1000 organizations, the 1000 largest publicly traded companies in the United States, they demonstrated not only a strong connection with multiple financial performance and effectiveness measures, but something else equally important: that these practices *preceded* performance by *three years. The effect after three years was much stronger than that found when performance was measured concurrently with the introduction of HPMP.* This is what would be expected if HPMP had served to *cause the improved performance*.

The Lawler study above demonstrates the usefulness of *gathering data over different time periods*, in order to move closer to the core focus of much of this research: *to demonstrate an element of causality between management practices, morale and performance, flowing in that order.* Many researchers have to tiptoe around this issue because they did not gather data over time, as Lawler and his colleagues did. Another study which faced this issue head-on was conducted by four academics at the University of Maryland.[26] They tapped into an employee opinion database which had been collected by a consortium of large US companies over many years, whereby the companies shared the data on some of the questions in order to have a "norm" against which they could all compare themselves.

The researchers used a "slice" of this data covering an eight-year period and employed factor analysis to produce "factors" or groupings from statistically related individual employee opinion questions.[*]

---

[*] The authors state that the factor analysis, which can group together highly correlated employee responses to multiple questions into one factor, was necessary because not all of the companies in the consortium used all of the available "pool" of approved questions, or changed questions from year to year. The factors allowed for a more reliable measure against which to compare performance outcomes.

Such factors included satisfaction with security, satisfaction with pay and so forth.

As predicted, they found:

- *Significant correlations between overall job satisfaction, the job security and pay factors over **multiple time lag periods**, with financial perform-ance (specifically Return on Assets-ROA and earnings per share-EPS).*
- *Especially significant from a statistical viewpoint, satisfaction with pay was shown to be a strong predictor of ROA over one, two, three and four year time lags, and of EPS over two and three year time lags. This means, for example, that the satisfaction with pay questions were answered between one and four years before the ROA or EPS measure was made.*
- *A surprise came, however, when they looked at the reverse direction: they found an even stronger correlation over multiple time lag periods between external performance and the security factor than the other way around. The connection between pay and external (financial) performance was almost equally strong in both directions.*

Logically this might make sense in that employees working in a successful organization would experience a greater sense that it would continue to be around for a while. Higher pay could also come as a result of good organization performance or could cause better performance, as others have also suggested and demonstrated.

In the book entitled *Corporate Culture and Organizational Effective-ness*, Daniel R. Denison followed the financial performance of 34 publicly traded companies for five years after having surveyed them on morale-related questions at the beginning of the study. Interest-ingly, while short-term financial performance was improved in those companies where employees reported that a greater focus was placed on morale-related HR practices, *it was the focus on participative management in particular which correlated most strongly with steady improvements in financial performance* in the companies over the five-year period.[27, 28]

Employee satisfaction and engagement compared to later-measured business unit outcomes

While most of the studies we are presenting here use a general measure of employee morale, which some call satisfaction, as their basis for comparison with performance outcomes, one large study[29] extends this to include the engagement index which we have discussed earlier. One of the authors being from the Gallup organization, this is not surprising: Gallup's increasing emphasis has been on its proprietary 12-item engagement questionnaire, called Gallup Workplace Audit (GWA). The overall satisfaction level of employees was measured by a single questionnaire item.

The study was a *meta-analysis*, or combination of studies, of 7,939 business units in 39 companies across many types of industry, involving almost 200,000 employee respondents, and the outcomes measured were customer satisfaction, productivity, profit, employee turnover and accidents. One other part of the methodology was particularly valuable: *the performance results were gathered later rather than concurrently with the employee opinions*. The deliberate goal here was to test the *predictive power of employee satisfaction-engagement data for later business unit results*, a test which was successful.

- *The findings are powerful for those arguing for a morale-performance connection: after statistically correcting for various possible errors in measurement,* **employee satisfaction and engagement correlated with composite business-unit performance at 0.37 and 0.38 respectively.**[30]
- *Breaking down the composite performance measure into its parts, the most significant and strongest connections between the satisfaction and engagement scores were negatively with employee turnover, and positively with customer satisfaction-loyalty, and safety.*
- *Of special interest, the correlations between general employee satisfaction-performance and engagement-performance were almost identical. This shows that, at least compared to a one-question general satisfaction item, the 12 Gallup engagement questions (GWA) do indeed tie in well with overall morale.**
- *The authors suggest, as we highly recommend elsewhere in this book, that the results support the practice of analyzing one's own high performance business units to mine them for data on management practices which support and drive such positive outcomes. The enormous benefit of this is that the data is gathered from inside one's own culture, not a textbook or scholarly article. It is specific to one's own organization.*

---

* The important issue as to whether overall satisfaction-morale is fully captured by one question is one we will discuss later.

WHY MORALE IS SO IMPORTANT 2: INDIVIDUAL MORALE AND PERFORMANCE

As we stated in the Introduction, morale is something which exists at the individual as well at the group level. It therefore makes sense that it will be connected with and influence *individual performance* at work. A person who has a sense of personal well-being in relation to work, who is in the fortunate position of being more committed, more engaged, generally *more satisfied*, would be expected to work harder and be more productive.

Interestingly, the individual focus of this type of study was the overwhelming choice of researchers for many years; only more recently has the idea of group morale leading to group performance taken on significant importance.

In spite of all the research activity in this area and the apparent logic of a strong correlation as its core proposition, the study of the individual morale level and *individual* performance has been a rocky road over the years. Described as the "holy grail" in Industrial and Organizational Psychology,[31] the connection between the two was for a long time thought to be non-existent or at best, minor. Only more recently, thanks to the process of bringing together multiple studies into one and re-examining their data (so called "meta-analysis"), can we gain some clarity and answer the question more definitively. Thanks to this type of analysis, we do not need to take you through each individual study: someone else has taken the trouble to do that for us, something for which we are extremely grateful!

The biggest and best of this kind of analysis we are referring to was carried out in 2001 and involved no less than 312 studies of the individual morale-performance connection.[32] The actual phrase used is "employee satisfaction" however, which we can take to mean morale given the way the authors define and discuss it.* These studies in turn involved some 54,417 employees. This research brought up to date another meta-analysis which had been the "gold standard" in this area since 1985.[33] Not only did it capture almost four times the number of

---

* The authors use what they call a "multi-faceted" or general approach to defining job satisfaction: rather than using one facet such as satisfaction with pay, they examined (i) either studies which combined multiple measures of satisfaction from different aspects of the work situation or (ii) used a general measure contained in one or a small number of questions about overall satisfaction.

studies analyzed in the 1985 study, but it also, in a way that only academic research can do, devastated the conclusions which that study had reached, through careful criticism of their methodology.

- *Such was the effect of this new analysis that the job satisfaction-job performance relationship, which had been left almost for dead after the 1985 study, came back to life with a **resounding 0.30 correlation** between the two.*

We say this is "resounding" because the newer study *almost doubles the correlation which the previous "gold standard" meta-analysis had delivered (0.30 versus 0.17)*, and which had been widely quoted ever since its 1985 publication. As the 2001 authors point out, this is also well within the range of other well recognized and researched predictive measures of job performance such as assessment centers, focused interviews, etc. Especially interesting was the fact that jobs with more complexity had a stronger correlation between satisfaction/morale and performance: 0.52 for "high" complexity jobs such as scientists versus 0.29 for jobs of "low" complexity, which the authors define as clerical, etc.[34] This confirmed what has been known for some time: *control is a big factor in morale, the individuals having it are much more likely to experience higher morale than those without it*; and a high complexity job, by definition, will have more control. It is also one (but not the only) reason why "higher" level employees such as top management generally have higher morale than "lower".*

It also makes sense that this relationship is not one way: satisfaction/morale affects performance but once that performance has happened it also feeds back to satisfaction in a "job well done".

It may be asked why the correlation is not even higher. To begin with, a doubling is quite a good result for those of us convinced of this relationship and having observed it in many workplaces and in employee focus groups, but never seeing it show up in methodologically sound research. Having said that, it should be remembered that other factors come into play when human beings are involved in anything. The authors cover this in some detail, and we will summarize some of these other factors here:

- The first explanation as to why satisfaction and performance do not correlate 100 percent has to do with the "gaps" which exist in many

---

* This would also predict that mid management would have higher morale than those working for them, but this is not always true, for reasons we will discuss later.

areas of human life: as an example of this consider the field of intelligence, where there exists what is called the "competence-perform-
ance" gap. This is the difference between the *capability* of the
individual and what they *actually deliver* on a given day in a given
situation with a given intelligence test. Extrapolating to this situation, a given level of satisfaction or morale is going to be "mediated"
or "moderated"* by factors internal or external to the individual
before it becomes "performance". One of these could be *mood*, which
might be lower for any reason in spite of the overall, medium to
longer-term satisfaction or morale level. Coming between ("mediating") satisfaction and performance, mood acts to change the
outcome, i.e., the performance level.

■ Mood could also theoretically come into play in the reverse situation: a given level of performance does not lead to a *guaranteed* level
of job satisfaction. It travels through the mood of the individual
before it arrives there, and changes as a result. It also travels through
the personality of the individual, her values and beliefs, for example
her conscientiousness ... the list goes on. All of these have an effect
on the outcome.

None of this changes the authors', or our, conclusion, as to the
connection between job satisfaction and performance; and since they
define satisfaction in a general way which relates strongly to our definition of morale, we can conclude that morale has indeed been isolated
as a very significant factor in individual work performance. *Specifically,
it has been shown to have as much predictive power as any other widely used
work performance prediction method.* As we mentioned in our Introduction, after many years in the backwoods, this relationship has been
brought out into the light again. The authors of this valuable article
seem to have the same opinion as ourselves as to the importance of
job satisfaction and morale. They demonstrate this by quoting the
following from a third party:[35]

> Job satisfaction ... has been around in scientific psychology for so
> long that it gets treated by some researchers as a comfortable "old
> shoe", one that is unfashionable and unworthy of further research.
> Many organizational researchers seem to assume that we know all

---

* For a definition of these statistical terms, which sometimes get confused with
each other, look at the excellent discussion, with examples, on Wikipedia:
http://en.wikipedia.org/wiki/Mediator_variable

there is to know about job satisfaction; we lose sight of its usefulness because of its familiarity and past popularity.

WHY MORALE IS SO IMPORTANT 3: MORALE AND CUSTOMER SATISFACTION

Mary Smith is a top-performing saleswoman at XYZ Ltd. Mary wakes up one day in a bad mood after a restless night. She picks a fight with her spouse before heading out to work, where she will meet with 10 customers in the next 8 hours. How will Mary handle it?

■ As a professional who always attempts to leave her home life behind her when she arrives at work, she will do her best to cover it up and be the best she can be.

But what if Mary wakes up in a bad mood *every day*, because she hates her boss, does not think much better of the products she sells, and does not feel the sales compensation system or the handling of territories is fair. Will she also be able to handle this on an ongoing basis? Of course, Mary can look for another job, if jobs are available, but that is not always the case. Will Mary "take it out" on her customers in some way? Will her frustration show? In other words will Mary's personal morale come to affect her customer relationships and will that translate into dissatisfaction on their part? Since a salesperson is often the "face" of a company to customers, at some point the company itself and its products and services can become tainted by the image presented by one individual sales representative's behavior. If they have a choice of supplier, such customers may leave, since, as the sales seminars tell us, "people buy from people they like".

On any given day there are many Marys in salesforces around the world. Some are that way regardless of external circumstances. If they were offered a job selling an occasional cruise on a tropical island with a free beachfront cottage and a good salary, they would still complain! Not much the organization can do will ever change the way they are, and most salesforces try very hard to avoid such people in the first place or to remove them once they show their true colors (which may not have happened in the interview process). For the rest, the origin of their low morale is not in a permanently negative and disgruntled personality but in the culture of the organization, its management practices, policies and everything we have discussed.

The issue of salesforce (including sales service and anyone else with customer contact) morale and its connection with customer satisfaction is something more and more organizations take very seriously. If they don't, they are missing a major opportunity to tap the performance consequences of employee morale.

Does customer satisfaction really translate into better performance?

This may seem like a strange question, given the obsession that most organizations have with customer satisfaction. But is there real evidence that customer satisfaction has the performance correlates one would expect of it? Is there proof that satisfied customers result in greater sales, profitability, and ultimately higher share values? If we are to suggest that morale is a driver of customer satisfaction, then we need to answer this, unless we wish to be faced with the "so what?" question when we posit the morale-customer satisfaction connection.

The American Customer Satisfaction Index (ACSI) database and related research

The ACSI goes back to 1994 and is a publicly available source of information which many academics use for their research. ACSI polls some 65,000 consumers a year, by telephone. As *BusinessWeek* (US) reported in 2009,[36] the data in the index has been examined by Professor Claes Fornell of the University of Michigan, Ross School of Business, for signs of correlation with the stock prices of its component companies. Interestingly, Fornell is reported as finding that ACSI companies whose scores increased in 2008 had share prices decline by 30 percent, compared to 38 percent for the S&P 500™.* Companies whose ASCI customer satisfaction scores had declined, *saw their share prices decline much more: by 57 percent.*

The *BusinessWeek* article points out that the *predictive power* of this database was recently researched by a group from Vanderbilt University: using data from 1996–2006, the group found that

---

* The widely used benchmark "S&P 500" in an index owned and maintained by Standard and Poors, and tracks 500 of the largest market-capitalization companies in the United States.

simply buying all the stocks with high ASCI scores did not make for a winning strategy; instead, if an investor focused on those which had *increasing scores* over the past year and were above the national averages, the returns were of the order of 1 percent a month. *This investment strategy returned 212 percent over the 10-year period, while the S&P 500 gained 105 percent.* Since stock prices represent as clear a "value" of an organization as any other measures, it is clear that providing superior customer service appears to be a major value booster.

The IBM research

One of the companies which have done extensive research on this is IBM, which produces what it calls a Net Satisfaction Index (NSI) based on customer research. IBM found that for every point this index score increased, there was an associated increase of $5 million in revenue.[37] In the United Kingdom, Tesco is a good example of success through focus on customer satisfaction. In the late 1990s, it began a process of improving the customer experience which even included allowing the return of grocery items to the store, no questions asked. No one had done that before, in that industry. Tesco's focus paid off handsomely in terms of market share, profitability, etc.[38] Many other organizations which have made the switch to a customer-oriented culture have benefited from it in the same way.

One of the keys to this is that the most successful companies do not try to please all customers; they focus on the best and most profitable ones. As Mark Graham Brown points out in his book on the prestigious (US) Baldrige National Quality Award:

> Years ago many organizations spent huge sums of money to drive up customer satisfaction and found that it did nothing to improve sales or profits. The Baldrige (Award) criteria do not suggest that you need to build a relationship with all customers ... Solectron, a two time Baldrige winner which manufactures circuit boards and electronic components, managed to improve sales and profits dramatically while reducing its number of customers. It is hard for a growing organization to turn away business, but that is often the best strategy for ensuring profitable growth.[39]

Customer satisfaction and shareholder value

One of the best and most widely quoted articles on this subject came in 2004 with the *Journal of Marketing's* publication of "Customer Satisfaction and Shareholder Value".[40] The authors state that this was the first study of its kind to examine this connection; using a rigorous approach and industry standard measures of both variables,* the authors concluded that a strong positive relationship existed between them in a widely diversified sample of US organizations. In developing the main hypothesis, the article spells out a number of reasons why having satisfied customers should also lead to an organization having an enhanced share value, all of which are backed by empirical data in their own right: satisfied customers would be more easily retained; it would cost less to do business with them in future; they would be a more stable source of revenue going forward; they would recommend the organization's goods and/or services to others, and they would be more open to cross selling. Their conclusion goes much further than confirming the hypotheses which they had proposed by making a powerful statement regarding quantitative relationships between customer satisfaction increases and the shareholder value of companies:

> a 1% change in customer satisfaction ... is associated with an expected 1.016% change in shareholder value ... for a (large) firm with average assets of approximately $10 billion, a 1% improvement in satisfaction implies an increase in the firm's value of approximately $275 million. This effect would be much greater for larger firms or for firms with a stronger association between satisfaction and shareholder value.[41]

This finding is quite extraordinary in that it is saying that there is *at least a one-to-one relationship between customer satisfaction and shareholder value*. It is therefore little wonder that the authors conclude that these findings will be of interest to investors, who might wish to know the customer satisfaction ratings of their target companies, as part of their due diligence.

---

* The ASCI Database of 200 of the Fortune® 500 companies as the customer satisfaction measure; Tobin's q as the measure of shareholder value.

Customer satisfaction, employee factors and financial performance in the food service industry

With their format of multiple locations performing the same task, the restaurant and hospitality industries provide excellent opportunities for research into the employee morale-customer satisfaction connection. In an example from food service, Gupta, McLaughlin and colleagues[42] examined the connection between customer satisfaction, repeat-purchase intentions and restaurant performance in 300 outlets covering half the US states. Customer satisfaction reports were completed by some 80,000 customers. The authors found, not surprisingly, that delicious food at reasonable cost was strongly correlated with the intent to return, but a similar result was also found for *factors which were provided by employee behavior*: a cheerful greeting and attentive service. Furthermore, intent to return was a strong predictor of actual return to the restaurant by customers, not just something they said they would do at the time of their satisfying experience. The authors conclude that the payoff for providing an excellent dining experience leading to satisfied customers at the average restaurant in this chain would be on the order of an *additional 1000 customer visits per year and $1.3 million in revenue for just a 1 percent improvement in the customer "comeback" score*.

While we have taken only a short journey into showing the connection between customer satisfaction and financial performance outcomes, we believe that it is valuable to keep these findings in mind as we consider the earlier connection, that between morale and customer satisfaction. Knowing what we have just seen adds importance to the morale drivers, since it *demonstrates a bridge between morale, customer satisfaction and organization performance*.

The customer experience

At some point in most peoples' day, we are customers. What kind of customer experience do we have and on what does that depend? Is it only the morale of the person serving us? Is it also cultural? Can training play a role? Most likely it is some combination, since these factors are interdependent. For sure, culture has an effect, which is why the Parisian waiter has earned such a bad reputation, perhaps unjustly? Or why American waiters with the "have a nice day!!"

salutations have the opposite reputation of acting like one's best friend, but in a rote, trained way. Some European friends react as harshly to this perceived falseness as Americans do to the stereotype surly Parisian waiter; but our all-time favorite response to this from an American who visited Europe was, "I'd rather have a fake smile than a real scowl!"

Speaking of that scowl, waiters and waitresses in certain central European countries can have up to two years of training in how to set tables, different wines, etc., yet apparently little in how to really make contact with customers and treat them well. Is this not on the training curriculum? If it is, why do they often almost throw the food down on the table with little or no personal contact? On the other side of the Atlantic, training for such people often consists of a quick walk through by an experienced member of staff, followed by them being launched into the deep end. Many have no idea about wines and cutlery layout, but they know to smile!

From this mix of experience, individual personality, culture, training and treatment of employees by the organization, comes the customer experience, with morale playing an important part. But do organizations really pay attention to and focus on customer needs as much as they ought to?

Management focus and the customer

Ken Blanchard is an author, speaker and consultant well known for his book *The One Minute Manager*, which found great success in summarizing management theory down to the basics for a wide and busy audience. His team regularly polls organizations for insights into something which is crucial as background for our research findings here: whether companies are organized around customer satisfaction and loyalty, are measuring it in a consistent way and actually practicing what is preached on the subject in every management book. The most recent results,[43] in which some 800 mid to upper level line managers, HR and training VPs, directors and managers were surveyed, provide real food for thought:

- While three quarters agreed that customer service was an important focus area, *only 44 percent* actually had formal processes in place to achieve improvements.

- *Less than half* indicated that their frontline customer contact personnel were empowered to take action to resolve negative customer experiences.
- *Fully 57 percent* had never calculated the costs of losing a customer or client (as the authors point out, it costs 6–7 times more to gain a new customer than to retain an old one).
- *Fully 36 percent* said that they never or only sporadically measure customer satisfaction.

The Blanchard poll gives us a backdrop against which to set out research on this topic. Results such as those from the poll indicate that with such headwinds, many organizations will have a difficult time making "fans" of their customers. Nonetheless, some have done so, and have linked their customer experiences to the employees who serve them.

Research on the morale-customer satisfaction connection

In the next chapter, a case study takes the reader through the Hilti organization's experience of merging morale and customer data. Hilti had the advantage of using its own internal data in order to discover this relationship. Not dependent on textbooks or academic research, the company discovered what reality was for itself, avoiding the risk that what was found to be true in other environments might not be true for theirs. This could be the case when studies have been conducted in different industries or types of organization than the one in which one works; is the comparison then really valid? What about between for profit and non-profit? There are also questions of culture, even in the same industry, which in our experience differs so greatly from one organization to the next. This is the reason why we always recommend to clients that they take the time to make this connection for themselves as Hilti did, if they have the data and the resources to do so. Bearing this in mind, research can point the way to important connections, especially if there are consistent findings, which there are. We will examine some of the recent research here.

In a book chapter published in 2001, Wiley and Brooks[44] followed up on earlier work by one of those authors on so-called linkage research. This refers to studies of the relationship between the way employees perceive the way they are treated and what they experience in the organization and various "output" measures, such as customer satisfaction. Wiley had five years earlier produced a model of this relationship which used research conducted by that author and others to show *strong connections* between various organizational input and output variables; essentially, it linked the "inputs" of leadership behavior and the employee response to that behavior, with the resulting customer satisfaction and financial performance of the organization. In the 2001 publication, the research was updated in a very interesting way and supported a *causal connection rather than simply a correlation* between these variables: research using longitudinal studies[*] found that the connection between the employee "input" variable (morale in general or specifically as it related to customer satisfaction issues) was indeed related to customer satisfaction and finally to organization financial performance in ways which support a causal relationship. This is exactly what we found in the Hilti study and have discussed above.

The authors quote an extensive study by Bernhardt, Donthu and Kennet in 2000[45] of 382 fast food restaurants, comprising more than 3000 employees, and an extraordinary 300,000 plus customers. They found the same connection as the others have done as far as employee morale and customer satisfaction (when measured at the same time). They also tested their data using longitudinal methods and concluded that customer satisfaction and the financial performance of the restaurants were causally connected in the direction one would predict (customer satisfaction>profitability). Measuring these two data sets at the same time did not provide support for this connection.

In addition, one of the most interesting findings in the Wiley and Brooks work was that the strongest relationship was not between what we would call the "overall morale" of the employees but between the specific sales-related morale questions on the surveys which were used for measurement. These items fall into a category known in the

---

[*] A "longitudinal" study is one which correlates variables over different time periods, as was done with the Hilti data at the end of the study when morale was measured before and after customer satisfaction. Longitudinal studies allow for causal connection hypotheses to be tested, while "concurrent" studies do not.

employee survey industry as "climate for service"* and typically include such elements as:

- Customer focus of the organization
- Training for customer service
- Focus on quality
- Recognition for service excellence
- Teamwork and cooperation among employees
- Empowerment of employees[46]

In another publication, the same authors provide a quantitative example of the connection between employee survey questions which are generally oriented toward overall morale issues and those which are customer-oriented, as detailed in the "climate for service" list above. When those survey questions were correlated with improvements in customer service perceptions in an 800+ unit retail store chain, the actual correlations were twice as high for the customer orientation items in the employee survey compared to those focused on general employee "satisfaction". When analyzed further it was concluded that the customer-oriented employee survey items accounted for more than four times the variance in customer satisfaction scores, compared to the general employee satisfaction items.[47] However, while these correlations were powerful, they were not the main focus of this study: that was *sales growth*. This was shown to be not especially strongly correlated with overall customer satisfaction, but to *"service excellence"* by sales staff, and the best predictor of that was again the set of sales-oriented questions on the employee survey.

Researchers at IBM's Rochester, New York AS/400 facility also found significant positive correlations between several "input" and "output" variables.[48] Measurements were made in over 50 areas, broken down into three general topics: revenue and quality, quality-oriented such

---

* "Climate for service" is a phrase referring to a workplace environment which is oriented toward creating customer satisfaction through an employee focus on the elements mentioned here, as well as others. Typically researchers in this area refer to an alignment of *human resource and marketing activities, with manufacturing and other operational aspects of the organization* which, working together, enable employees to provide superior service to customers.

as customer satisfaction and warranty cost and people-oriented such as employee morale. Some of the correlations were extremely high, such as:

- Employee satisfaction with one's manager and satisfaction with the job itself: 0.92.
- Employee satisfaction with one's manager and general employee satisfaction: 0.92.
- Employee satisfaction and customer satisfaction: 0.70.
- Customer satisfaction and market share: 0.71*.

The strong correlation flow from perceived management behavior to market share is powerful. All that is missing is a longitudinal study which would allow for causation to be inferred from these results. In the meantime, though, they support the connections which we have seen in our own studies and extensively in the literature.

Sears Canada also found strong, statistically significant connections between employee morale and customer satisfaction but the study added a twist: *only those areas of customer satisfaction under the control of employees were significantly correlated.* These included solving customer problems quickly, having good product knowledge, ensuring short waiting time at cash registers, etc. No such relationship existed for factors not under employee control.[49]

WHY MORALE IS SO IMPORTANT 4: MORALE, INDIVIDUAL AND ORGANIZATIONAL HEALTH

So far in our examination of the performance benefits of high morale to the organization, we have focused on what it **brings**. There is, however, a completely different side to this story, which may be as or more important than what we have seen so far: *what morale prevents.* What if preventing something could enhance employee and organization performance? With this in mind we enter the world of individual and organizational health.

---

* The data in this Baldrige.com report are from an article by Steven Hoisington and Tze-His Huang at IBM Rochester.

The Swedish WOLF study: Management behavior and employee health

Consider the following study lead by researchers at the famed Karolinksa Institute in Sweden, in combination with medical scientists from other parts of Sweden, as well as from Finland and the United Kingdom.[50] We use this word of praise ("famed") to impress on our readers the high quality source of this research, and thereby to add to its credibility, because the findings were quite extraordinary: *they showed that the morale driver we have called the "boss from hell" can have an effect on employees' lives significant enough to increase their incidence of cardiac disease.*

Now that we have your attention, let's look at the study to see how it came to such a conclusion. By way of background, the researchers point out that their interest had been piqued by extensive data which one of them had helped collect, showing that an "adverse psycho-social work environment" could increase the risk of cardiovascular disease by 50 percent.[*] [51] They wanted to follow this with a carefully controlled study that drilled down into this environment from the general level to look at a specific factor in the causal chain. In this case, they theorized that management behavior could be one of those "psycho-social" stressors leading to negative outcomes for employees, a theory which we would certainly embrace given our contention that management behavior is THE leading factor in determining organizational morale.

Some 3239 men from Stockholm area employers were given a series of screening tests for cardiac health as part of the larger so-called WOLF study which also included women. This study was limited to the men because of the much greater incidence of ischemic heart disease ("IHD") among men generally, on which this study focused. The final study group size, after leaving out men older than 65 and those who already had heart disease, was 3122. Sweden being a country with an integrated national health system, health data were readily available for these men.

Their health history was followed for up to 10 years, and unlike previous studies which had been open to criticism for using more subjective ("self-reported") measures of cardiac events, the authors here took no chances and rigorously limited these to events proven by MRIs, CT scans, ECGs and enzyme tests.

---

[*] One of the authors of the study we are examining here had conducted the earlier "meta-analysis" of multiple studies which came to this conclusion.

The data on management behavior were collected from the men via a 10-question survey which included items on *communication, clarity of goals and expectations, whether the manager showed empathy for the employee and how he felt, whether the boss took time for the employee's professional development and whether the employee received praise for a job well done or criticism for the opposite.* For the actual questions the authors looked to a section ("leadership climate") of the previously published and recognized Stress Profile.[52]

Two stunning results came from the study:

- *Some 74 serious cardiac "events" such as heart attacks occurred during the course of the study;* **controlling for all other factors, the more negatively rated the boss was on the leadership scale, the greater was the chance of the employee having such a cardiac event.** *This was a statistically significant difference.*
- *That probability of a cardiac event increased with the time the employee spent at a particular organization.*

While an immediate reaction to this second bullet might be that this was because time on the job is correlated with age which is correlated with heart disease, we repeat that age and all other risk factors were controlled in this study, in order to isolate leadership behavior. Another reaction to this bullet might be that an individual might have more than one boss during a 10-year period in the same organization. This may be true, in which case the results may have to be explained in another way:

> We would suggest that the culture which hires and fails to identify or modify the negative behavior of the "boss from hell", and leaves this person in place, is likely to have more than one, and probably many! In other words, even if an individual in this study did move jobs in the same organization, he (the study was all men) might find himself once again up against a similar individual in a leadership role.

With morale driven by leadership behavior in many of the areas measured by this short survey, and leadership behavior capable of creating such devastating outcomes to employees, the authors suggest that intervention is necessary to create a healthy work environment for employees. Interestingly, they use data from their research, which showed that *certain questions about managers were even more predictive of cardiac events*, to suggest that emphasis be placed especially *on providing employees with sufficient information necessary to do the job and sufficient power for their responsibilities.*[53] We will return later to the profound significance of this statement as we examine ways to create and maintain the high morale culture.

Is this study typical? Does a manager really have such power to affect peoples' lives in such a way that their *good health is supported or compromised*? If so, this would widen our scope considerably and expand the effect of individual and group morale well beyond issues of the financial performance of an organization or the satisfaction of its customers. It would give an expanded meaning to the phrase "driving performance" from the morale improvement process. Other studies give us further evidence that the answer to these questions is YES.

"Justice" at work: The Whitehall II study

The concept of "justice at work" is widely used in academic literature but rarely heard in executive suites or among groups of employees, especially in the United States. The former may have reason to avoid such a topic, given some of the inequities that exist in compensation, especially in the United States, between line workers and top management. In fact, even to bring up such a word might result in grumbling about "socialism". Line employees in every country may not use the word "justice" per se, but they certainly use other words which convey the same meaning or form part of what justice implies: *fairness, equity* and so on. Europe's generally more equitable work culture is a more welcoming place for this concept than the United States, and justice at work in some form or another is often codified into law, such as the requirement that German firms of a certain size all have a *Betriebsrat*, or works council, which has Board representation. This is quite separate from any union to which they might belong.

As we have already briefly mentioned and will later stress even more in this book, the justice or equity factor is a powerful driver of organizational morale. Its effect goes much further than that, however: as this next study shows, justice at work is correlated with the cardiac health of employees, as measured by incidence of coronary heart disease (CHD), *the leading cause of death in Western societies.*

The study[54] involved some 6442 individuals in the United Kingdom, taken from an ongoing research group* of civil servants called Whitehall II. Justice at work was measured by a short (5 item) questionnaire containing items on whether the employee had *experienced unfair criticism, received consistent and sufficient information with which to do the job* from his supervisor, felt that his supervisor *listened to his problems* and whether he experienced *being praised for a job well done*. The men were divided into *three justice groups* based on this data: high, medium and low.

As in all studies of this type, various demographic and risk factors were measured in order to be statistically controlled. These included health measures such as *cholesterol levels, level of physical activity, hypertension and body mass index (BMI)*, and demographics such as *age, marital status, educational level and employment grade.*[55]

The researchers also use questionnaire items to measure what is called *"job strain"*, which is a combination of factors relating to the relationship between the *demands of a job* combined with the *amount of control* which the employee experiences while doing that job. As one of us told clients on many occasions, without the insight which academic research provided on this subject (most consultants have little time to read such things), nothing is worse or more stressful for most people than a job which places extraordinary demands and either lacks control or a clear direction. *"Effort-reward balance"* was also measured, being a ratio of the two where rewards are not just pay but also things like promotions, social approval and job security.[56] Having these two factors in the database allowed for control of these variables and isolation of "justice" as a key driver of the health issues which emerged in this group. The questionnaires were administered multiple times over a three-year period during the study, which averaged 8.7 years of follow up. A long follow up, such as in this and the previous study, is necessary to provide more exposure to the development of cardiac events.

The findings were again impressive:

- Some 250 men in the study had incidents of coronary heart disease (CHD) during the 8.7-year follow up.

---

* Such groups, called "cohorts", or groupings of individuals sharing certain characteristics, can exist over long periods of time and be used as research subjects in multiple studies. Whitehall II is one such cohort.

- Both before and after adjusting for all risk factors, high justice at work was associated with a *lower risk – 30 percent lower – of CHD* than the medium and low justice groups.
- Job strain and effort-reward imbalance were also associated with higher CHD, **but not in the high justice group.**
- The effects were not dependent on *job grade or socio-economic status. Administrative, clerical and executive grades* were equally affected by the justice level and its relationship to CHD. This is interesting in the context of evidence that workers who are at lower levels in organizational hierarchies experience 3–4 times greater risk of CHD.[57, 58]

As the authors point out, job strain and effort-reward imbalance have been connected with CHD in several studies, but here we see what appears to be a **mitigating or protective effect of justice at work taking place, lessening the negative effects of the other two factors.** Justice is also something which is completely dependent on management behavior, unlike job strain and effort-reward, which can include external economic factors such as labor market conditions. As such, the combination of justice's importance as shown in this and other studies, and its dependency on management, means that we have identified one of the key morale – and employee health – factors which can be improved by changing management behavior.

To be fair, challenges have been made since this article was published[59] as to the extent which one can truly infer causality from management behavior to health in this situation: specifically, using any form of self reporting can be problematic due to the biases which it introduces. Self-reporting was of course used to measure justice at work in both the studies we have examined so far. Of course this is often challenging in the social sciences, but it should be noted that it was at least avoided on the outcome (health) side of the equation in both studies by use of medical tests rather than self-reporting of cardiac events.

Secondly, as some of the original authors of this Whitehall II study readily admit,[60] the concept of "justice at work" does overlap with other related psychosocial factors, making it difficult to say that specifically that one factor is the causative agent. For sure, more research can and must be done in this valuable area: these are still early days in the quest for connections between specific aspects of work life and health.

Job strain, effort-reward imbalance and health

As we mentioned in our review of the Swedish WOLF study, both job strain and effort-reward imbalance were measured and controlled statistically in order to attempt the isolation of the effects of justice at work. The reason for the need to isolate them from justice is the fact that they have both been shown to be potent predictors of health risk at work in their own right.[61, 62] It is also a fact that there is some overlap between, say, effort-reward imbalance and justice: if the reward for hard work is not there, is there not an element of injustice experienced by the employee? For that reason, the WOLF study found that as justice went up, effort-reward imbalance went down,[63] as would be predicted by the example just given.

This is very interesting from a morale point of view because between them, job strain and effort-reward cover such morale-related items as: job demands, compensation (especially variable compensation such as piece rates and bonuses), performance reviews, promotions, job security and so on. As the research shows, all of these factors at work are related to the health of the employee.

Bad boss day, anyone?

The phrase "bad hair day" has come into the vernacular over the last few years. How about a bad boss day? We have all had them, but do they have health consequences? One small study[64] in England gives us a fascinating insight into this issue, looking at lower level female employees who were employed as healthcare assistants. Many of these women reported working for two different supervisors on different days.

By giving the participants a questionnaire related to how the saw their supervisor's management skills, *especially in the area of fairness and equity of treatment*, the researchers were able to produce two groups for the project: one of the groups, which acted as a control, worked for only one supervisor or for two for whom she felt about the same, according to her responses on the questionnaire. The second, experimental group, had two supervisors for whom the feelings were quite different: for one supervisor they were positive and for the other, relatively much more negative.

The study's researchers did not tell everyone involved about the true nature of the study, because it would have affected the results.

They were given only general information, within common ethical standards for such research.

The blood pressure of the participants was checked at work every 30 minutes, and also at home on non-workdays, to provide a baseline. When the results emerged, *the blood pressure of those women when they were working for the less favored supervisors was significantly higher than for the control group and for their* **own** *pressure on days when they were working for the supervisor for whom they had positive feelings*. The differences were so great (systolic pressure of 12mm of mercury (Hg) and 6 mm Hg diastolic), that the author of the study makes the point that these numbers are associated with greatly heightened risk of CHD and stroke. He emphasizes that point by asking how physically risky it must be for those people working all day and every day for a highly dysfunctional boss.

A fascinating part of the research was that for the experimental group, the drop in blood pressure on days when they worked for the favored supervisor was even greater (although not significantly so) than when they were at home! Perhaps the sheer relief and contrast of being at work without having to suffer under a "boss from hell" made this happen? Another part of the study confirmed what we saw earlier: a specific set of questions from the array given to participants, that referring to *fairness of treatment by the supervisor*, had the greatest predictive power for lower blood pressure scores.

Predicting sickness absence from morale-driving factors

Our research review so far suggests a role for certain elements of morale drivers, specifically the "justice at work" aspects, in the health of workers. It is not much of a stretch therefore to hypothesize that having things like more equality and fairness in one's work life would lead to less sickness absence, and vice-versa. This is exactly what a Finnish study[65] discovered: looking at over 5000 healthcare employees in 7 hospitals in that country, 4076 of whom (mainly female) completed a questionnaire on justice in the workplace, the study showed that sickness absence was greater among those reporting lower levels of justice, for both men and women. The sickness absence was measured not only by self-reporting but also medical records of the individuals concerned.

Sickness absence was not the only health-related outcome measured; after controlling for other factors, justice at work again correlated significantly with positive health outcomes, and status in the hierarchy of health care jobs (from doctors to clerical workers) did not make any difference.

The Healthy Organization

The studies relate to a field of research referred to as the *Healthy Organization*.[66] In our first chapter of this book, we made the point that, especially in Europe, organizational morale is often referred to as *"well-being"*, which in the United States is much more focused on physical health. This demonstrates that there is, *in the language*, an intersection between the psychological state of employees and their physical health, and for good reason. As our research examples demonstrate, they really do interact: if a person at work is in a poor state of morale brought on by some condition at that job, that can affect his/her health. It follows that an organization which can maximize morale across a large percentage of its workforce can also improve employee health, reduce health care costs, reduce absenteeism and what is called presenteeism (where an employee is present, but barely able to function such that she might as well be absent). An employee who wakes up one day and realizes that his job is stressful in this way is also a candidate to leave the organization and add to turnover costs. Being a healthy organization, from the psychological and physical perspective, then translates into financial health through control of these important costs. This is additive to the many benefits which morale brings to financial performance in the other areas we have discussed.

Conclusions: Morale and worker health

It has long been the case that Western societies have measured and regulated the workplace physical environment to protect the health of all who work there. The studies we have looked at give a fascinating view of the emerging evidence that our work *social* environment can also have health implications. The morale connection here is quite clear, even if social science does limit what can be researched and

105

how: *various elements of how people are treated at work, specifically related to fairness and equity and the balance between effort and reward, have strong health connections,* **and these are independent of other established work stressors.**[67] While parsing out which specific element is THE one which makes all the difference may be difficult, it seems to be clear that a combination of them can have very positive or negative effects. The interesting part here is that *exactly some of the key elements which contribute significantly to a high or low level of morale among a workforce are those which these researchers from medical institutes and departments in universities isolate as the key factors in the health connection.*

The performance effects of morale's health connection are clear: we may not be talking about earnings per share or customer satisfaction numbers – yet – but we are talking about the physical health of employees and all the hard and soft costs related to that. If high morale can act as a protective force against such negative effects, that is a performance factor in which it is well worth investing.

WHY MORALE IS SO IMPORTANT: CONCLUSIONS

We began this chapter with a series of statements about the impact of morale on an organization, some of which were based on our own experience. Knowing that our readers might find that interesting but also would be looking for proof of such broad ranging effects, we have attempted to demonstrate in the last four sections of the chapter, exactly what has been discovered about the morale-performance relationship.

Our journey into the research which has been generated on this subject has taken us from the huge employee opinion databases of the international consulting firms down to the smaller studies conducted around the world by academic researchers. We started out with a conventional view of performance in terms of *financial measures*, we moved on to *organizational effectiveness outcomes* and then looked at *the customer satisfaction connection*; we then branched out to an area in which high morale appears to have a preventative performance effect, allowing the organization to stay in good "shape", *employee and organizational health*.

Our conclusions from all these studies are quite clear, and our own beliefs about morale, based on experience in the field, are confirmed: research shows that the importance of morale is much greater than that of a "nice HR exercise" designed to give "good feelings" to the employees of an organization. We can say unequivocally:

*Morale has a huge impact on, and is a **proven driver** of, organizational performance:*
- *At both the individual and the group level*
- *In both private and public sector organizations*
- *From financial to customer satisfaction measures*
- *From organization effectiveness and productivity to employee health*

Morale touches and affects the most significant performance aspects of every type of organization; a high or low morale level helps empower or disable the organization's ability to achieve its goals.

CHAPTER 4

CASE STUDY: CULTURE, MORALE AND CUSTOMER SATISFACTION: HILTI GROUP, SCHAAN, LIECHTENSTEIN

Note: Our case study organization was chosen with three criteria in mind:

- *It should have created a demonstrably **high morale culture**, proven by employee surveys.*
- *This culture should have **endured over time**. We did not want a "flash in the pan".*
- *It should have **won national or international awards** for its efforts in this area, demonstrating that it is recognized by industry peers or by specialized outside organizations as setting a particular standard of excellence in the area of morale.*

Most people are familiar with the red Hilti vans with the distinctive block letter logo, which drive from one construction site to another to assist customers. The company is based in the idyllic surroundings of Schaan, Liechtenstein and is a world leader in providing technology to the construction industry, for example in fastening systems. If you drive on a motorway or over a bridge today, or work in a high-rise building, chances are that Hilti products had something to do with it. Construction workers treat its tools and materials with the same reverence that motor mechanics have for the Snap-On brand, and architects specify Hilti brand tools and materials be used on all sorts of construction projects. Founded in 1941, the company is privately held by the Family Trust named for its late founder, Professor Martin Hilti, and currently has 21,000 employees. Revenues in 2008 hit CHF 4.7 billion.

Hilti has been surveying those employees for many years and is known for its progressive human resource policies and practices. For a seven-year period until 2002, one of us had the opportunity to conduct these worldwide surveys of its employees. We found that morale was not only always high overall but continually improving, and reflected the values of the organization in textbook fashion. As we have said before, however, this never comes to pass without continuous effort on the organization's part. To demonstrate this effort and the importance of a high morale culture to Hilti, consider this summary of the company's annual results in a recent year following our research, by Michael Hilti, Chairman of the Board at that time:

> It is not products that make a company lastingly successful; it is people – the environment in which they work and the culture that shapes that environment. The fact that we have always cared strongly about people and corporate culture has nothing to do with philanthropic inclinations, but plain and simply with the cultivation of one of the most, if not the most important driver of our business success.
>
> Integrity; commitment in the sense of responsibility and obligation; courage to leave behind established habits; teamwork – for around twenty years now, we have anchored these essential corporate cultural values through systematic worldwide training, requiring great personal and financial engagement. And this applies at every level: porter, Board member, team leader, production employee. From Schaan to Shanghai.
>
> I believe that there are two points in connection with this where we differ from other companies.

1. Full commitment at the highest levels of leadership. Every level of the company, including the Board of Directors and the Executive Board, goes through the culture training. All four Executive Board members are integrated and involved in leadership training as moderators and participants. Each of them invests at least ten days a year in training. They demonstrate as well as live their commitment – and can thus directly influence the course of training.
2. The knowledge that corporate culture is not a temporary project, but an integral part of the company's day-to-day stability. Many companies see the establishment of corporate culture as a project or program, like re-engineering or quality improvement. No: the development of corporate culture is a journey without end! Right now, we are rolling out a further developed version of our cultural

training with the name "Our Culture Journey". Here, too, the Executive Board was the pilot team for the first trial of this new version – and last week the Board of Directors also concerned itself with this training.

Bear in mind that this was not a presentation designed to focus on human resources, it was *the* annual report for shareholders and the financial community. In printed form this presentation took up 5 ½ pages of which *fully half were dedicated to culture, customer satisfaction and employee morale!*

In 2003 the Carl Bertelsmann Foundation awarded Hilti the prestigious Carl Bertelsmann prize; its theme was *Corporate culture and leadership approach as success factors.* This further burnished its image and reinforced its people-centered culture.

Like many companies, Hilti also surveys its customers on a regular basis. As is the custom, that data was at the time of this study managed by sales and marketing, and the employee morale results were the territory of HR. We wonder how many companies are like this, keeping two powerful databases separate from each other instead of combining them? Our guess is perhaps 80 percent or more.

One day while one of us was discussing this with top management at Hilti, the idea was born to merge these databases and mine them for information on three key questions:

- Which factors contribute the most to morale at Hilti?
- Is there a relationship between customer satisfaction and employee morale in this organization?
- If there is a relationship, is it the same between people who have customer contact and those who do not?

If Hilti knew the answers to that first question and could then show that morale and customer satisfaction were related in their company, and with which employee groups, they had a complete picture of *both the morale drivers and the end result. Knowing this, they could target management training, promotions, rewards, and other interventions to the specific areas identified as being most highly correlated with morale, thereby increasing their chances of ongoing morale improvement and the resulting customer satisfaction.*

When the answers to these questions came back they were quite stunning, and resulted in a presentation which the CEO at that time,

Dr. Pius Baschera, took around the world to various venues, and for which he received significant positive feedback. The results only reinforced what Hilti had already suspected and added some valuable new information.

METHODOLOGY

At the time of this study* there was some limited academic research which showed connections between customer satisfaction and employee morale, but Hilti wanted more information which was *specific to them*, not something out of a textbook which might or might not apply to their culture, management practices, market position, etc. A project was started which would pore through years of data from customer surveys, conducted around the world, and the matching years of morale data *in the marketing organizations*. Later, pre and postyears of employee morale data were added, to test the hypothesis that the relationship might differ when tested from a different time perspective; indeed this was found to be the case, and allowed for some causative conclusions to be drawn.

With a network of marketing organizations around the world (currently 120 countries in which there are 200,000 sales contacts made *per day*), and with each of those organizations doing more or less the same activity (both sales and support), Hilti presented itself as an ideal candidate for research of this kind. With so many locations and each one being surveyed for employee morale once every 18 months at that time,♦ as well as for customer satisfaction every 2 years, the amount of data was plentiful and the ability to correlate this data much enhanced (the ability to correlate two factors depends on the number of data points, in this case surveyed locations). The fact that the data went back for many years also assisted the project: we could then look at customer satisfaction and employee morale for the same time period or stagger them to test various theories. For example: morale first, customer satisfaction two years later; customer satisfaction first, morale two years later.

---

* Data was collected for an initial stage of the study from the 1995–7 survey periods then analysis was extended up to and including 2002 for a second phase.

♦ Hilti currently surveys its employees worldwide every 12 months.

Identifying morale correlates

One of the most powerful analyses one can do with employee survey data, along with creating an overall morale score and ranking groups, is to correlate individual questions with that overall morale score. When this was done at Hilti, it showed that not all questions are created equal: what we called their "power factor", their ability to predict the overall result, varied significantly. Some questions had extremely high correlations with that morale score, which is interesting when one considers that we were correlating one question result with the average score from an overall questionnaire total of 100+ items.

To start the process, Hilti first asked us to focus on questions in several areas which were of particular concern during the period in question, and on which the company had been focusing some change efforts. This was useful to the company because it could then test whether these efforts were appropriate, or guide them to a new direction. The following were the areas of focus and some of the specific questions within those areas:

- Size of the marketing organization being studied.
- Basic attitudes toward the company and job.
- Communication.
- Productivity.
- Employee involvement/empowerment.
- Mid-level management.
- Pay.
- Job security.
- Supervisory relationships (multiple factors related to how the supervisor is seen as treating the individual).

The Hilti marketing organization ("MO")

The typical Hilti MO staffing in a particular country consists of TSRs ("territory sale representatives"), CSRs ("customer service representatives") and (HCRs) ("Hilti Center representatives"). There are also some support staff who do not have much or any customer contact. The MO headquarters for a country would typically have several satellite "Hilti Centers", where customers could receive technical support, return tools for service, purchase supplies, etc. Most TSRs work out of their homes with occasional visits to MO headquarters. In terms of *direct customer contact*, the TSRs have significantly more than most CSRs and Hilti Center Reps. This turned out to be very relevant for the study.

Results: Morale correlates at the company

Most of the items studied, and listed above, correlated with the overall morale results of the Hilti surveys; but some had much higher than average correlations. The initial result, however was a surprise: *knowing the size of the marketing organization ("MO") in a particular country, one would have no possibility of predicting its morale score.* As the Chart 6 below indicates, the data are like a "shotgun" across the page, with no adherence to the trend line, and no significant correlation.* This is interesting because some in the organization adhered to the theory that a smaller MO would be easier to manage, and allow for a more intimate and effective relationship with employees, etc. As we had found out in other organizations, however, this was not the case.

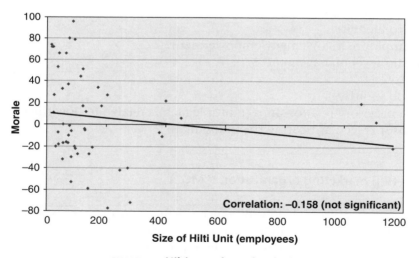

CHART 6   **Hilti morale and unit size**

_____

* Each dot on the following charts represents a Hilti marketing organization in a specific country. A morale index score of zero represents the average morale score for all of Hilti.

This was not the case for the other questions, and those having to do with management had especially strong correlations. For example, consider the following chart (Chart 7): it shows that in an MO where the employees see their supervisor as encouraging suggestions, there is an extremely high probability that overall morale will be good. In only 5 cases out of 1000 would this be a result of chance.

The same was true for MOs in which employees gave high ratings to local management ability (see Chart 8):

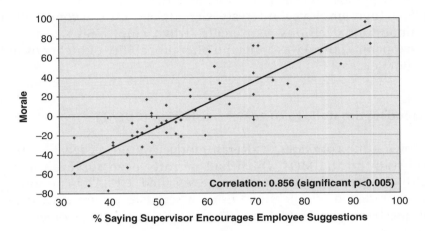

CHART 7   **Hilti morale and supervisor seen as encouraging employee suggestions**

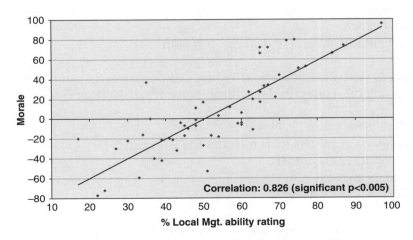

CHART 8   **Hilti morale and local management ability**

At the end of the study, Hilti had information which suggested that not only the above but also several more questions correlated highly with overall morale. These included:

- Quality of overall communications received by employees (better communication was correlated with high morale).
- Duplication of effort as seen by employees (greater amounts of duplication were correlated with poor morale; this was an issue with overlapping responsibilities in some territories).
- Whether employee interests were taken into account when important decisions were made (when employees saw this as happening, there was a much higher probability of higher overall morale).

Extending the study to customer satisfaction (CUSAT)

Knowing the correlates of overall morale, we proceeded to extend the study to the MOs which had recently been surveyed in the Hilti customer satisfaction process called CUSAT. The survey was conducted by telephone using a script to ensure consistency of questioning.* CUSAT focuses on three aspects of customer satisfaction:

- Willingness of customers to repurchase from Hilti.
- Whether customers would recommend Hilti to others (so-called advocacy).
- Overall satisfaction of dealing with Hilti.

Using a statistical process, it reduces responses of customers to the following categories, in descending order of satisfaction:

1. Hilti "Fans"
2. Bonded Customers (this includes the Hilti Fans)
3. Comparing Customers
4. Endangered Customers
5. Nearly Lost Customers

---

* The customer satisfaction data were not conducted by our organization but by an internal Hilti unit.

Our interest in the research was to look at the most enthusiastic "Fans" and the larger group of Bonded Customers which included the Fans.

We used data from a two-year period of conducting customer satisfaction surveys (Hilti calls their process CUSAT), and this gave us a total of 21 MOs with which to work. The first run of the data consisted of correlations of results for the same time period, that is the customers and the employees had been surveyed in the same calendar year.

Results: Customer satisfaction

The data were presented back to management in a question and answer format combined with supporting graphics. The results began with overall results for the MOs, then moved into specific job groups:

Overall Marketing Organization:
Q: Do MOs with higher employee morale have more satisfied customers than those with lower morale?

A:
  – MOs with higher employee morale have a significantly greater probability of having Hilti "Fans" in their markets.
  – MOs with higher employee morale have a significantly greater probability of having Hilti "Bonded Customers" in their markets (Bonded Customers include "Fans").

Sales Force ONLY:
Q: Do MOs with higher *salesforce (TSR, CSR, HC Reps.) morale* have more satisfied customers than those with lower morale?

A: MOs with higher *TSR morale* have a significantly greater probability of having Hilti "Fans" and "Bonded Customers" in their markets. *The relationship between "Fans"/ "Bonded Customers" and TSR morale is greater than that for the total MO workforce, or the combined group of TSRs, CSRs and HC Reps.*

It was the last part of this finding which especially captured the attention of Hilti's top management: *it showed that the more contact the sales employee had with the customer, the*

117

higher the correlation between salesforce morale and customer satisfaction. The TSRs, with the most contact, had the strongest connection. The non-sales support in the MO had the least correlation with customer satisfaction, and the combined salesforce was in the middle, exactly as one might predict.

The chart below (Chart 9) shows this in a much more easily understandable format. The bars represent correlations of the two customer groups, "Fans" and "Bonded Customers" with Hilti salesforce employee morale. The most customer contact is experienced by the group on the far left, territory sales representatives and, sure enough, they have the highest correlation. This is followed by the larger group of TSRs/CSRs and Hilti Centre Reps, with a lower correlation. The least customer contact is experienced by "MO: Non sales", who had the lowest correlations of all MO groups.

Also of extreme interest was the fact that, when only Hilti's most engaged and committed customers (the "Fans") were taken into account, the correlations with MO morale scores were much greater when the MO employees had customer contact than when they did not. In fact as the chart below (Chart 9) shows, non-sales employees who worked in the MO (for example, secretaries who had little or not customer contact) *had a morale to "Fan" customer satisfaction correlation half that of customer contact employees.*

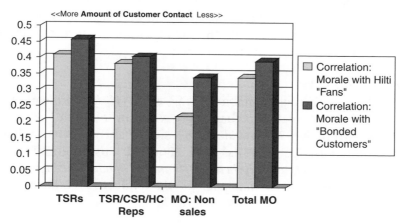

Note: "Bonded Customers" include "fans"

CHART 9 **Morale of different employee groups and % of Hilti "Fans/Bonded Customers"**

When seen in the context of our previously detailed research which demonstrated particularly high correlations for the specialized "climate for service" employee survey items with customer satisfaction, our Hilti study is all the more powerful because it used *overall morale measures and not just the climate for service items*, which are much more specific. It appears from the Wiley and Brooks data that had we done so, the correlations would have been even higher than what we found. However, this was very deliberate, since we were looking to support the Hilti practice of making a high morale culture for *all employees* central to its competitive strategy, and we attempted to support the importance of overall morale, which is what happened. It should be remembered, too, that general employee morale questions often cover issues which are critical to the strategic competence and values of many organizations, even if they correlate somewhat less directly with customer satisfaction. Should a significant drop in some of these non- "sales-oriented" survey results occur, *it might be in areas where damage could occur to the culture of the organization*, which in turn surely could affect customer perceptions and satisfaction.

Which comes first? Customer satisfaction or employee morale?

When former CEO Dr. Baschera took these results out on the road and showed them to executive groups, he received very positive feedback, but also some questioning as to whether the connection moved in an opposite direction than that which he believed: from employee morale to customer satisfaction. While correlation is never cause, it was assumed by both the Hilti team and us as consultants that this was the correct assumption, but a reverse assumption could also be supported. In that direction, customer satisfaction and enthusiasm for Hilti products would feed back to employees, especially TSRs with whom they had the most contact, and make them feel good about working for the company which made such good products and offered superior service.

On receiving this feedback we went back to the data and extended the study. The results were analyzed using the following formats:

1. Testing employee morale in an MO up to two years **before** the collection of customer satisfaction data for the most engaged customers ("Fans") at that location.

2. Testing employee morale in an MO up to two years *after* the collection of "Fans" customer satisfaction data at that location.
3. Testing employee morale in an MO at approximately the same time as the "Fans" customer satisfaction data had been collected.

This data shown in Chart 10 below produced findings which were as powerful as the original correlations:

- *Employee morale correlated **most highly** at Hilti when measured before or concurrently to the customer satisfaction survey, **for all MO groups**. This difference was statistically significant. As our model of morale > customer satisfaction would predict, the highest correlations would be in the "Up To Two Years Before" relationship between these variables, and that is exactly the finding for the Total MO and all but one sub-group, as Chart 10 clearly shows.*
- *Employee morale correlated **least highly** at Hilti when measured up to 2 years **after** the customer satisfaction survey. If employee morale "drives" customer satisfaction rather than the other way round, one would predict exactly these results.*
- *If there is some feedback from satisfied and enthusiastic customers which makes the employees "feel good" then we would also predict a non-zero*

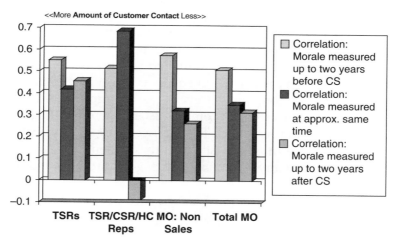

CHART 10   **Effect of time on morale-customer satisfaction correlation: Hilti "Fans"**

*correlation in the direction of customer satisfaction>employee morale, but a lower one than our primary driver of employee morale >customer satisfaction. We found exactly that **in every group**.*

■ *Our model predicts that having the most customer contact would facilitate the **strongest positive feedback loop** from customer to employee, and that the TSRs would therefore show the highest correlation between morale and customer satisfaction among all MO groups **when morale is measured after CS**. This is also exactly what we found.*

Overall conclusions of the Hilti study

Hilti was able to draw some powerful conclusions from the study:

■ *Hilti sales organizations in which the employees say they are treated positively by management and supervision in just a few clearly definable ways have higher morale (**across a broad range of issues**) than those in which this is not the case.*

■ *In Hilti sales organizations, higher employee morale (especially among those with direct customer contact) is correlated with higher customer satisfaction; the more customer contact, the stronger is this statistical relationship.*

■ *The highest level of engaged Hilti customers, so-called Fans, have a customer satisfaction level which is double the correlation with sales-contact employee morale in the MOs, compared with the correlation with employees in that MO who have little or no sales contact.*

■ *At Hilti, high or low employee morale **precedes** similar highs and lows in customer satisfaction, significantly more than the converse.*

■ *Because of this connection, Hilti's strategic practice of putting people first was strongly reinforced: not only does certain specific activity by management drive higher morale and provide the many other benefits we have discussed in this book, but **results in** greater numbers of more satisfied and enthusiastic customers.*

The findings could be expressed in two simple graphics (see Figure 3) which show the positive flow from *specific aspects of management behaviour*, through to higher morale and finally to customer satisfaction:

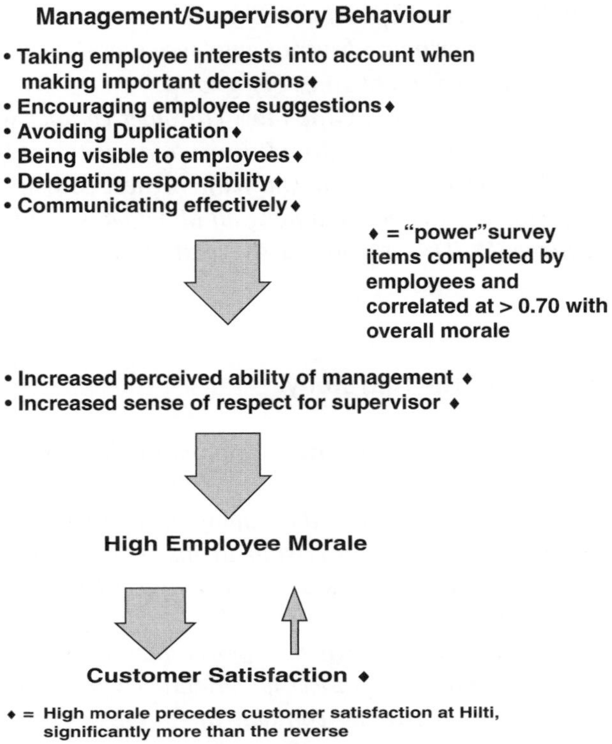

Management/Supervisory Behaviour

- Taking employee interests into account when making important decisions♦
- Encouraging employee suggestions♦
- Avoiding Duplication♦
- Being visible to employees♦
- Delegating responsibility♦
- Communicating effectively♦

♦ = "power"survey items completed by employees and correlated at > 0.70 with overall morale

- Increased perceived ability of management ♦
- Increased sense of respect for supervisor ♦

High Employee Morale

Customer Satisfaction ♦

♦ = High morale precedes customer satisfaction at Hilti, significantly more than the reverse

FIGURE 3   Hilti's positive flow: From management to employees and customers

As Michael Hilti put it in the same annual report quoted above:

Since we not only measure employee satisfaction but also customer satisfaction, we are able to show strong correlations between the two. They reveal that management behaviour according to our values positively influences employee satisfaction and working morale. A Hilti organizational unit with a high degree of employee satisfaction usually has a higher degree of customer satisfaction and works more profitably than units with lower rates of employee satisfaction.

Management behaviour according to our values drives employee satisfaction and working morale. Employee satisfaction and working morale drive customer satisfaction and loyalty. This way, we initiate a virtuous cycle – generating sustainable profitable growth. Result: *People and corporate culture are not "soft"* *strategy elements but substantial drivers of our business results and one of the key secrets of our success.*[*]

INTERVIEW WITH HILTI'S CHAIRMAN

Dr. Pius Baschera, formerly CEO of Hilti, is now the Chairman. As someone with a long involvement in the company's cultural and morale efforts, he was our choice as interviewee when it came to adding some background to, and placing, the Case Study data in context.

Q: *Pius, you've got such a long history at Hilti of success with people, morale has been high for a long time. What do think Hilti's basis of success is with this high morale? How do you do it?*

A: Why do we have so much success on the people development side? I would say that it all starts with a vision from the owner of the company[♦] and the top management at the time – that was in the 80's – to formulate or define a culture in the company that they would like to have that is based on clear values. Not just defining that, but making sure that it's lived by the top of the organization, and that it's connected with the key business processes, like for example, an HR process of people development. Not only lived and integrated, but also that we are consistent in the company that if people are not living these values, even if they are excellent results producers, if they are not living our culture and our values, that we are consistent and that we are separating from these people. Let me just say the next important thing is that we are measuring the development of living this culture, the development of the employee satisfaction of this company in a periodic way because there you see what you have launched in 1985 in creating a culture and defining a culture and living a culture and integrating it and in being consistent and you know that is really creating results. OK? So it's a really very consistent approach from defining to living to integrating to measuring and reacting on the information.

Q: *Yes, you just said something very interesting, "when somebody doesn't live this", even though they are a good performer, you have to "separate*

---

[*] (emphasis added)

[♦] The term "owner" refers to a Family Trust and until 2000, partial ownership by external shareholders whose shares were traded on the Swiss stock exchange. The Trust now owns 100 percent of Hilti.

from them". Now do you think it's easier when you have a strong people orientation to make these hard decisions, for example, to fire people, or is it more difficult because you are a people-oriented company, and does a people-oriented company fire people like this?

A: I would say the other way around. It makes it much easier because you know we have clearly defined things not just on a piece of paper, but based on our cultural trainings, cultural workshops. We have a new development now with workshops we call *"Culture Journey"* that we do every 18 months for all 20,000 employees, so it's so clear for every-body in the company what we would like to have as a culture in the company, where values are important. So many cannot say "I didn't know that", it's so clear and you know, I often hear that this is the soft factor stuff, but this is not soft at all. I think if you clearly define what culture you want, how you want us to deal with each other in the company, and if somebody is going against these rules, then I think it's much easier to separate from somebody than if you would not define that and then you have to argue a lot. For example, you know that we have the value of "integrity": lets say we have an issue that goes against this value; if its not so clear that it is one of our values and that we're serious about it, we will be in a defensive position now and in the future. In our mind, you know, defining a culture, living values, these are hard facts, very hard facts and in the case of people not behaving according to that, we have to react, and this is understood in the organization very well. I can give you a very short example, you probably have heard it and we often explain it to our employees and those on the outside the following way: we say with our strategy that it is defining the playing field, where we would like to play, and with our culture, we define the rules of the play. So we can use that and lets say our strategy is that we play American football, and the rules of play are our culture; and if Roger Federer, our top star in tennis, joins our American football team, and runs with us with his racket onto the football field, we have to tell him, you know, "the rules are American football rules; please go back to the cabin, change your tennis shoes and your racket, and come back in the clothes you need for this game; and if you don't want to do that, then please look for another team; perhaps a tennis team and go on a tennis court!" So this is a simple example, but it's very well understood.

Q: *It's very good. I didn't hear that particular example before. Pius, maybe sometimes when you go on your journeys and because you're on the Boards of other companies, people might say to you, "Well Hilti has a great market position, financial success ... you can afford to be so good with people, it's maybe a bit of a luxury, but we can't do that" What do you say to someone who says that?*

A: (Laughs). A nice American word would be. BS! Look this is completely crazy if somebody said that, because think of our experience. We know that very excited and motivated people are driving customer satisfaction; you have it in your book, in your (Hilti data) example. If you know that, how can you say "we can't afford it?" Who could afford not having enthusiastic customers? So it starts not with the customer, but with having motivated employees, the motivated employees are creating enthusiastic customers. So every company, even if its in crisis, has to make sure that its people are motivated, and know the direction of the company from a strategic, and also from a cultural point of view.

Q: *Let me ask you something that I struggle with at times. It's a question of when you promote people, and you've got somebody who is technically very good, and maybe this is the Roger Federer example, but let's just see. You've got somebody that's technically very good, but maybe they are not the best "people person". How do you balance the need for the technical knowledge with the people skills? And would you make preference for the people skills, if you had to make a choice? Would you go with the people side in every case?*

A: OK. I would say for leadership positions, we clearly go for people skills, development skills, compared to the technical skills, but you know we have many positions in our company where we need technical experts whether its in IT, in research, development functions, where people development skills are not really in the center of this job. Where we would still be strict here is where we're looking for technical people or specialists and they're not adhering to the values of integrity, for example, or courage, OK? Also if they lacked team orientation, we would have a problem with these people also, even though they're not in a managerial function.

Q: *Pius, I just pulled off the Internet this piece about you cutting the work hours at a couple of your plants in Liechtenstein as well as planning to do the same at plants in Germany and Austria. Obviously you are affected by the world economy quite a bit. Can you give me a sense of how morale fits in to what you're doing there and why you make that choice, and how you think it will affect things?*

Q: Well, yes I think it's especially in these times, in these crisis times, people will watch how we live these values now, how we live our culture. Will we for example stop running our cultural training workshops because we can save the money? How did we communicate the short working hours, how are they introduced, I mean this is very important now for the trust of the people that these values, this corporate culture is not just OK for good times, but also the way we want to lead the company in bad times.

So are our people excited that we go for short working hours? Certainly not. On the other hand, how we explained it to them ... you know we had ... I don't know if you know that we closed our plant in Tulsa several years ago, five, six years ago, and we announced this closure 1 ½ years before we closed it. Now you're in the U.S. environment, normally you don't do that. It's a much shorter time notice, so we did that and as far as I know, everybody in the staff found a position internal to the company or external, or went into retirement. So this is the culture, how we do things, we're open, we're direct. We informed the people early enough, and did they like that we closed the plant? No, certainly not. But also the image in Tulsa, in our hometown in the U.S., did not deteriorate. In fact the other way around because everybody had seen, aha, you can also take these tough decisions and put them into practice in another way, in a way that is living the culture in difficult times.

Q: *One of the theories in the book is that morale could be, in exactly this situation you describe, almost like a protective shield in difficult times, because you have this people orientation. Is that the way you see things?*

A: Are you saying that this cultural work that we did over the last 20–25 years would help us now to protect against a crisis? Is that the question?

Q: *Yes, exactly.*

A: I would say that we created a foundation that people trust us in management; that people know that what we say, we really mean and we do that also. So this culture, well we have these values, but it's much more ... it's that management is visible, management is touchable, management is predictable and this, especially in crisis time, is a very good foundation for people to accept those changes because they know its needed, it's openly communicated. They know they trust the management, that they have done the utmost to avoid the very tough measures. On the other hand, if tough measures are initiated then they understand it is really necessary, and then its done in the Hilti style.

Q: *Many thanks Pius.*

CHAPTER 5

CREATING/MAINTAINING THE HIGH MORALE ORGANIZATION: DO WE *CREATE* HIGH MORALE – OR STEP OUT OF THE WAY?

Some organizations already have high morale without any purposeful effort to reach that point. An especially charismatic leader, a fortunate market position (Google comes to mind), a small start-up with a lot of excitement, expectations and young, idealistic founders and employees ... all these individually or in combination can have a powerful effect on morale and represent very fortunate circumstances for everyone involved. It is part of the reason why such organizations seem to rocket to success out of the blue; not just the new technology of a breakthrough search algorithm as in Google's case but the added driver of morale which brings loyalty, almost limitless enthusiasm and engagement. In these examples there are clues as to what is possible and we can learn much from them, but what percentage do they represent of the organizational universe? It's not such a big one, and means that for the rest of us there is work to do!

An important question here is the one with which thoughtful managers grapple: do we actively create high morale or do we create the conditions which would allow all the enthusiasm, commitment, engagement and motivation in our workforce to come out, if we only just *step out the way*? If you go to enough HR seminars you are bound to hear this strategy sooner or later: the build-up is the list of wonderful things which are waiting to pour out of your workforce. The obstacle is management, which uses its levers of power to keep the creative spirits of the workers in check. It's a very compelling argument, especially if you work in the depths of some organization and long for freedom from meetings, management memos, obligatory reports, etc. There is no doubt too that significant layers of management really do act as a sponge which soaks up everything around it, to make itself seem valuable and important and all the other reasons which add nothing to organization effectiveness. Freedom from all this makes a lot of sense.

Having said that, though, our answer to the question of simply stepping away is :

Not So Fast!!

What we mean by this is that, if you can answer all the following questions in the affirmative, by all means, go ahead and step away. Otherwise, there is work to be done:

- Have you created the right culture for a high morale organization (in terms of the way you do things)? Bear in mind that this culture involves having in place the processes which support it and which are based on appropriate values and guiding principles.
- As a crucial part of this culture have you done the work of finding the right people and putting them in the right jobs?
- Have you gone top to bottom in terms of your management and HR practices and made sure that they all support this culture and your stated values?
- Have you gone to your workforce, measured how well this is working (not once but multiple times), listened intently to this feedback, and fine-tuned your organization and its processes to ensure the maintenance of high morale over an enduring time period?

If you can affirm these questions and have taken many of the steps we detail below, then yes, you might be able to step away, let your workforce loose and enjoy the fruits of your labor. But simply stepping away before you have diagnosed morale in your organization, before you know where you are starting from, stepping away while all sorts of dysfunctional practices are in place, is a recipe for disaster. Would you build a house without having someone carefully examine the basis on which you are building? Perhaps it is sand? That would be the equivalent of stepping away without doing the basic work needed, the structure we call the *high morale culture*.

The high morale culture

The building of a high morale culture follows a logical sequence which we have found is essential to a successful outcome. Like in medical treatment, a solid diagnosis is the basis of everything which comes later. But one "treatment" is not appropriate for all; organizations are in different places as far as the following:

- Whether or not they have started down the road to measure and improve morale.
- If they have started down that road:
  - how much they have accomplished with morale improvement and maintenance efforts, if anything; this includes the current level of morale.
  - what opinion employees have of the *process* and its utility.
- Whether or not they have started down the road of morale improvement: how much they want to or *can* accomplish, i.e., the question of implementation.

The question of implementation

Let's go back to our conversation between the doctor and unfit patient who wants to run the London Marathon and extend that with two other patient scenarios:

- Our original patient can barely make it walking around the block. His chances of running the London Marathon are slim but not impossible with great physical and mental effort. Even then, physical limitations may prevent him from reaching his goal. Time is also crucial; he might not make it this year.
- Patient number 2 comes in, is already able to run half marathons in decent times, tests well in terms of cardiovascular fitness, has a good height to weight ratio, etc. She is told she is in fine shape to enter the Marathon.
- Patient number 3 might have run half marathons or 10Ks but found that it strained her, and testing showed that she had various physiological limits which had been reached.

Each one of these represents clients with whom we have worked. Many are in decent shape for a short race, but have Marathon goals. Can they make it? Others are far worse off. We have advised some organizations that, based on the "shape" they were in from a people perspective, the outlook was cloudy. Their strategy looked good but the implementation potential was low. Their choice then became one of changing goals, or going on a major internal change program which may or may not be successful.

Changing goals is not always an option, however: for some it is change or cease to exist. An example of this would be when an industry undergoes a huge shift, as in deregulation or in the move from government ownership to stockholder ownership (perhaps also involving moving from a monopoly position to a competitive one). In the United Kingdom, the United States and on the European continent one can find examples of this with the automobile, energy (electric and gas), coal, steel, railway, telecommunications, airline, postal and other industries. During the 1980s the electric utility industry in the United States was deregulated and component parts split off from the whole (generation, transmission, wholesale and retail delivery). One of us had been studying the industry for some time, from a cultural and morale perspective, and we had data which showed that the industry looked to be in woefully poor "shape" for the changes on the horizon.

One day we were asked to make a presentation to the top 500 managers in a well-known and successful utility company, and the participants sat in silence and some fear as they saw the gap between the entrepreneurial future which faced them and the current, far from entrepreneurial culture and morale profile which they shared with most similar companies, and which their survey data had highlighted. The CEO then stood up and told them of the huge changes their company would immediately start to make to meet this challenge. In the end, they became a winner in this situation, buying others which did not face up to what was needed or were too slow to do so. Many utility companies disappeared.

Such a change is possible even in a company which has had decades in which it is wedded to an older, very different culture. But it can be so daunting for some that the cultural shifts cannot be managed with current management and many of the employees, who signed up under "different rules" will hang on to "the good old days" for perhaps decades until they retire.

Implementation and the Accenture studies: A wake-up call

Since much of the initial efforts related to morale measurement and improvement begin with the "people people"-HR, it is valuable to see what shape they are in, in the eyes of their "customers", the internal users of their services. It is also valuable to see how executives see their *overall* organizations' readiness to undertake efforts related to building a high performance, high morale culture. Accenture, the international consultant and outsourcing specialist, has studied this for some time and regularly updates a survey which it conducts in several countries on what it calls "*The High Performance Workforce*".[1] For the latest study, conducted in 2006, some 251 executives (CEOs, CFOs, HR and Training Heads, CIOs) were surveyed in 6 countries and 5 major industry groupings.

Beginning with the overall view, consider the following result from this study: several key factors were selected by the Accenture respondents as being *crucial for financial success*; yet when asked how well their organization was addressing these, there was often a huge "delta" or gap, as the following table (Table 4) shows:

TABLE 4   **Accenture performance factors**

Top 4 key Factors in achieving strong financial performance	Rated "very important"	Rated "addressed very well"
Building strong customer loyalty	59%	**26%**
Acquiring new customers/ increasing market share	61%	**21%**
Having a performance-oriented mindset in the workforce	41%	**18%**
Attracting and retaining skilled staff	45%	**17%**

Source: Data from Accenture: reproduced with permission.

At this point it should be clear that all four factors above have a strong morale element; this has been demonstrated in our chapter on performance and customer satisfaction. This study extends that data to the question of implementation, and casts a poor light on that question, indeed. These high level respondents should surely know about the state of their organization if anyone does; yet they respond at the rate of only 17 percent and 18 percent respectively that their organization is currently "addressing well" the crucial issues of attracting and retaining skilled staff and having a performance-oriented mindset in the workforce. Two critical factors relating to customers are not much better implemented, either.

In terms of HR's and other groups' "image" with these individuals, it calls into question some serious implementation issues, as the following table (Table 5) shows:

TABLE 5   **Accenture "Most Important" functions**

Functions considered one of three most important in organization	% Selected	Rated performance as "High"
Sales	62%	25%
Customer service/support	43%	25%
Strategic planning	23%	33%
Finance	23%	19%
Marketing	21%	37%
Engineering	20%	29%
Human Resources	**19%**	**19%**
IT	17%	26%
R&D	16%	33%
Manufacturing	14%	36%
Training and development	**9%**	**14%**
Logistics	8%	26%

Source: Data from Accenture: reproduced with permission.

If Accenture's data in any way reflect the state of one's own organization, there is work to be done and caution to be exercised in the implementation of morale improvement programs. If HR really is seen by only 19 percent as one of the "top three" functions in terms of importance to the organization, *and is rated at the same percentage for its performance*, we should all be wary of delegating too much in that direction until we know how things stand where we work. Of course, a well-designed employee survey can and should have questions in which internal "customers" rate the different functions such as HR and will allow you to decide where and how to best implement the changes we are about to discuss.

The question as to whether HR deserves the image it has from such as the Accenture survey is a good one. But does HR arrive at that point under its own steam or because of the way it is treated, structured and staffed? It seems that for far too long, Human Resources has been the "cost center" which "can't get any respect". Even recently, we find serious articles from distinguished academic authors like Professor Edward Lawler which ask everyone to give HR more consideration, and offer a better way forward which might raise its profile and ratings:

> Imagine a company in which the human-resources department has great talent and technology and advises top executives on business strategy and organizational effectiveness. It has a say in big decisions and is a critical career stopping point for anyone who aspires to senior management.
>
> Sound like a foreign concept?
>
> That's what an HR department *should* look like in a company that considers its work force to be its most important asset – a major source of competitive advantage.
>
> While most companies say they value human capital, in reality, few are run that way. They may have systems in place for hiring talented people, but their organizational structures aren't designed to develop, motivate and retain the best ones. And the group with the expertise to help the organization better manage and utilize people – the human-resources department – often is too mired in administrative tasks to tackle higher-value work.
>
> In a company built to leverage human capital, the HR staff would spend less time processing benefits requests and more time being the expert resource on the state of the organization's work force and its ability to perform.[2]

The author goes on to suggest that HR free itself by outsourcing its more mundane functions, in order to focus far more on the strategic functions detailed in the last part of the quote.

Even in the roles where it could be effective in moving the organization toward higher morale, therefore, HR has sometimes been unwilling, unable or not permitted to push for such efforts. Stuck with a less than stellar image (deserved or not), or mired in other activities, there has been no time, *no focus on such things*; and it must be said that in some cases, HR has been staffed with people matched to the more mundane rather than the strategic.

Bearing all these important factors in mind, our prescription for organizations will therefore depend on their starting point and the "shape" they are in overall and by major function (and certainly not *only* HR). The distinction must also be made between those which are venturing for the first time into the morale improvement area, those who have worked with morale before but would like to make a "new start", and those who are already *successfully* underway and wish to continue in the same direction.

STEPS FOR THE NEW OR "NEW START" USER OF MORALE IMPROVEMENT PROGRAMS

Step 1. Making high morale a strategic imperative

Organizations which have no history of working on themselves in this area have good news and potentially bad news:

- *The good news is that there is no history of morale programs which did not work, or botched surveys that remain in institutional memory and which dull the desire among employees to ever share their opinion again. The slate is clean and one can do things the right way.*
- *The potentially bad news is that, never having measured or worked with morale, one might be the recipient of bad results. Was the reason that morale issues were ignored until now the fact that management suspected something was wrong but hoped that it would "just go away"? Or perhaps someone there subscribed to the pre-Neanderthal philosophy "it you don't measure it, it doesn't exist".*

Whatever the case, the opportunity here is to develop a solid program which will provide lasting benefit to the organization. The first step is one of commitment: If there is no commitment to high morale as a strategic imperative from the very top of the organization, *it will not happen.* Of course we have argued that this move makes perfect sense because the benefits which flow from it are so great. It seems like a simple decision; but as we will see, there is more here than at first meets the eye.

More than anything else, leadership is required to inspire, cajole and convince employees, to actually demonstrate and embody for them the commitment made. By "employees" we do not mean just the line staff: mid-level managers and supervisors should be on the frontline of receiving and giving out communication about this process. Bringing people around to the point that they want to make the changes necessary to create the high morale culture is the key goal. Talking about it is not enough, just putting nice words into the Annual Report won't work; doing it is what it takes. Witness the Hilti *Culture Journey* program, it is mandatory for everyone from the CEO and Board of Directors to the most humble position in a factory or office. Leadership is so important here that putting together the many years we have worked in this field, we can confidently say the following:

> We have never seen an enduring high morale organization where the CEO (or whatever title that individual has) and each and every member of top management was not ***totally and completely committed*** to morale as a strategic necessity, requiring constant attention, resources and commitment.

Consequences

Once this commitment is made it has significant consequences: the organization may have to be structured, managed, populated and measured in different ways than before, and there may be resistance even among some members of the top ranks. If the difference between where the organization is now and where it wants to be is great, leadership will be significantly challenged to bridge that gap. This is why when this commitment is contemplated, it is enough to prevent some from moving forward; or once it is made, it is not carried through.

Step 2: Communication

In the high morale environment, each person knows what the values of that organization are and that its mission includes having a high morale workplace. Sometimes a phrase is used to communicate this mission, such as "Putting People First". Employees know that they should attempt to fulfill this mission and live by these values every single day, because they are aware of why high morale is important: not only does it make them feel good for 8 or more hours a day but it gives their organization a strategic advantage against its competition. How do they know all this?

- All of it has been thoroughly communicated to them.
- From their time working there, it becomes clear that this place is a far better one to work than almost any other they have experienced, and they wish to maintain that.
- All that they have been told is embodied in the way that management behaves toward them, demonstrating that the communication they received was not just empty words.

Step 3. Making it everyone's responsibility, not just HR's!

With good communication and follow-through, *developing a culture of high morale becomes the personal mission of every individual in the organization.* They wish to "embody" the values and behaviors which lead to this because it has a great positive effect on their daily life. This sense of *responsibility* means that if there is a "mobbing"* incident for example, non-management individuals get involved to stop it because they know that mobbing goes completely against the values which the organization wishes to maintain on an ongoing basis. Another example (but one at a management level) would be that if there is a downturn in business, there is not an immediate "knee jerk" reaction like a layoff; that would violate the stated values of the organization.

The Accenture data at the beginning of the chapter will probably give pause to anyone starting out on this road. It is clear that having totally committed top management is necessary but not sufficient to this process. Even with that in place, and in spite of its image problems which we have discussed, the building and maintenance of morale in the workplace is often "delegated" to an internal group such as HR. Common sense would dictate that, as they would *theoretically be the organizational "champion" of anything to do with morale.* But there are several problems with this, and they go beyond the capabilities of HR itself which we have discussed:

- Building and maintaining high morale is not an HR "program". It is a responsibility which starts at the top but involves every single

---

* "Mobbing" refers to the situation when people gang up and harass individuals at work. This term is used in Europe but might not be familiar to US readers.

individual in the organization. "Top down" does not work for morale; instead it should be called "inspire and lead from the top but create and maintain at all levels".

One of the main findings of our research and that of others shows that management makes all the difference as to whether one has high or low morale, more than any other factor. Our previous example of the two hospital Emergency Rooms which scored at opposite ends of the morale spectrum comes to mind here: the manager was really the only difference between the two departments. But the daily transactions between team leaders, supervisors, managers and those they lead cannot be "micro-managed" by HR; in addition, most managers have been hired by their own subunits, and HR has had little to do with that, except to make sure that legal aspects were covered.

- The biggest morale factor of all is therefore mostly out of HR's scope.

We are not saying here that HR doesn't play a role: for example, the compensation practices which they design and/or install can have a big effect on morale. HR also typically selects (perhaps also develops) and maintains training programs for managers.

- Finally, if HR is given the "project" to improve morale, the message gives others in the organization the impression that "HR is handling that"; in other words, they themselves have nothing to do.

This is the wrong message. Our most successful clients in this area make it clear to managers and all employees that morale is not being "insourced" to a particular group. *For all organizations, managers, especially, can and should be held primarily accountable for morale*, and all employees should be made to feel that they too are crucial to the organization's culture.

Consequences

Our conclusion is that HR may have a role to play in the sense of bringing morale and culture issues to the attention of top management if these issues do not already occupy that mental space, and providing some resources along the way (the HR senior executive may or may not already be part of the senior management group, which is another issue). But for the reasons we have set out, this goes far beyond that one department and should become part of everyday life for all in the organization.

We would strongly reinforce the ideas presented in our quote above from Professor Lawler, that in many cases organizations can and should benefit from a move toward a much more strategic HR, requiring different and new skill sets and, most likely, people. While we still would push hard on the idea that morale is everyone's business, an HR "upgrade" would give the morale process a boost from the more strategic focus of the HR group. For example, HR could answer crucial questions which managers have about morale in their groups, a key role which has them acting as internal consultants. If HR still reports at some lower level in the organization too, that represents a clear sign of the value placed on the function by the organization. Maybe you "put people first" but you "put HR third" in levels down from the top! Concurrently with the HR "upgrade", bringing HR into the executive suite (if not already there), or whatever the top tier of management is called, is a powerful recognition of the importance of people in the organization.

Step 4. Measurement: Knowing where you are now

There is a question which we receive more than any other, when we meet people and they find out what we do:

*"What is the **one thing** I can do to improve morale at my workplace?"*

We usually reply by asking a question:

Do you know how your morale is now?"

The decision to take the path of change will begin by learning from where one is starting. Imagine setting off on a drive to somewhere but not knowing the starting location, and having no GPS navigation system! It sounds absurd, but so many organizations do this with morale: someone reads a book, finds out what the "latest and greatest thing" is in this area, and demands that it be implemented starting next week. The journey has begun but the starting point is unknown and the destination is unlikely to be reached. (This is also known as the *"Ready, Fire, Aim"* style of management). For example, the team is dispatched on an Outward Bound* course designed to bond them, when in fact they would be quite well bonded if it were not for the new compensation system which has them competing and fighting with each other, instead of focusing on customer needs. A survey would have revealed this and anything else they needed to know before they took action.

We have discussed morale measurement in-depth well in advance of this chapter precisely because knowing the starting point of morale is the key issue to consider before anything else. The organization which is new to this area will probably want to go with an experienced research consultant to help them successfully measure their morale standing, and more than likely will choose an employee opinion survey. The data thus collected will be available as a "baseline" benchmark against which all change can be measured in the future.

The new user of morale measurement will want to take advantage of all the tools we have described, such as data analysis software and techniques. This will provide the tools necessary to look deep into the organization for morale issues, to create rankings like those we have detailed, etc.

Following the communication steps after a survey, the organization arrives at the point where change has to be planned and implemented. At this point, the new user of morale improvement efforts and the experienced user merge onto the same track. Both want to know what works and what does not, whether HR programs can and should be fine-tuned to produce the desired effect, or whether the morale improvements they wish to see have little to do with HR issues (such as compensation) and more with overall cultural issues like management style (whether at the top or at all other levels). Even before that though, there is a need to perform some form of organizational "triage", making decisions about change based on urgency, and expected outcome.

---

* Outward Bound and similar outdoor programs are a wonderful tool for team morale building, under the right circumstances; these include knowing exactly what one needs, based on a well designed morale diagnosis.

STEPS FOR ALL USERS OF MORALE IMPROVEMENT PROGRAMS

Step 5: Making decisions about change

The starting point, the current state of morale, will give you the key to knowing the answer to a binary decision which takes place at this point:

Leave it alone or change it

Sometimes "leaving it alone" is the best step, even if an aspect of morale is poor. This would be appropriate in the following circumstances:

- Maybe "it" is not a strategic point of concern, perhaps your resources would be much better focused elsewhere.
- Perhaps the organization simply cannot change "it" at this time, and more ground work needs to be done.
- Perhaps you do not have the right people in place to change "it".
- Perhaps events external to the organization (like a financial meltdown which occurred in Japan in the 90s or recently in the United States) have influenced morale and you cannot change them or their effect.[*]

Leaving something alone, or delaying it for now, can be a cleverer solution than doing something which fails and sets you back.

But let's assume you have done the diagnosis, and things look good, does it follow that when morale is shown to be at a high level, there is nothing to be done? Consider this situation which happened to one of us:

Meeting with a top management of a service company, one of the biggest in the world in its field, some data were presented about management morale. The data had been analyzed on a percentile basis, whereby one could see at what position this company scored on these management questions, versus an external database. When

---

[*] Being "in shape" to face such a crisis is critical: using the medical model, it is a strong immune system which can survive attack. Assuming an organization is already doing well in the area of morale though, major outside events can test it to its limit. Even well managed Japanese firms were tested this way during the "lost decade" financial and societal crisis.

told that they were at the 95th percentile, indicating that only 5 percent of managers from companies in the database scored higher than they did, nearly all the senior managers took on a rather self-satisfied look. Except for the CEO: with an urgent look on his face he jumped up and rushed to the screen, where he prodded at the chart being displayed, saying: "I want to know what the other 5 percent are doing"

He was reinforcing one of his core cultural beliefs: that there is always room to improve, and we can never rest on our laurels. This demonstrates the effect of the culture, and the top management drivers of that culture, on decisions to leave things alone or to change them. Some will never accept leaving anything alone. Not everyone will shoot for perfection, nor it is always the right thing to do; but some CEOs are wired for perfection and nothing less will satisfy them. Deciding whether to work for such an individual, and the extent to which you share this personality trait, will effect your individual morale, for sure! One thing was certain, though: the company had grown by leaps and bounds on his watch.

Knowing where one starts and deciding whether to change something or leave it alone is the first step. If it were that simple, though, everyone would do it, and they don't. That is because another factor is at play here: the organization's *willingness and ability to accept change*. By "organization", it sounds like it has a life of its own and we have again anthropomorphized it; while in the final analysis nothing in the area of morale exists except in the individuals who comprise the organization, there is also the observed reality that that "organization" can, because of its history, its past and present cultures, and various complex internal dynamics, appear to be a separate entity with its own actions. This has lead to the study and extensive literature in the academic field of "Organizational Behavior".

These factors are ignored at one's peril. This is the reason why one sometimes sees a very gung-ho CEO coming into an organization and failing to really change the culture of poor morale; never underestimate the mysterious forces which can be lined up against such a change! But they are not insurmountable, and sometimes (as in dreams where one confronts frightening entities only to find they are "paper tigers") they turn out to be easy to overcome. What is needed is a certain type of leadership; without this, change will not happen.

Step 6. Making changes: "Upgrading" management

If we have learned one thing from many years of working in this field, it is contained in the following, *the most important statement we will make in this book*:

Management is the key to high morale. Under most circumstances, everything else pales in comparison.

A definition here is important: although top management can have a huge impact on morale (see below), it is not top management with whom most employees have much contact.* It is the local or department manager, supervisor, team leader or whoever has the power to hire, fire, carry out performance reviews, grant salary increases and/or bonuses, etc. For us, *that is the key relationship related to morale:* for the average employee, their morale will depend more than anything else on *how they are treated by that person*. We know this from hundreds of surveys we have conducted, with many hundreds of thousands of responses from employees around the world, specifically:

The one question which is correlated most with overall morale is that in which the employee rates his or her manager or team leader on a general question. Many times we found extremely high correlations between this one question and the average of the other 100+ questions. In other words we could often predict the outcome of a survey for an individual or a group based solely on that one question.

It follows that making a change, a "management upgrade", has more effect on morale than anything else. To illustrate the power of management change on morale, consider this real-life example

---

* Small businesses, start-ups, etc. have an advantage here: entrepreneurs who are business founders have the chance to shape a high morale culture from the start if they can bring the right values and practices into the workplace which support this culture. Being able to keep in close contact with all employees, knowing them and their families by name, often socializing with them on weekends etc., enhances the team effect, provided the founder/entrepreneur is skilled with people in ways we will discuss. If on the other hand that person is unskilled or unwilling to create a high morale culture, things can be worse than in a much bigger organization, because there is no one else to whom the disaffected employee can turn.

which has repeated itself more than 100 times just in our consulting experience:

On completion of a survey, a particular location is found to be very low in morale compared to its own previous data and to the current organization-wide score. A change is made in management, and when the next survey is completed (in 12–18 months on average), the results are dramatically different; score increases of 20 percentage points are quiet frequent, where only +10 is a very significant change. Financial and operating performance of the unit almost invariably improves as well.

This type of change can be within a small group of only 10 people or among a much larger division of the organization, say a group of 200–300 people.

Although it is more often smaller management changes at the local or departmental level which affect the average employee, some examples of management change produce results so quickly and across such large organizations that it doesn't seem possible, and yet it is. The stock of Starbucks dropped precipitously over a period in 2008, and customers started deserting the formerly "must visit" caffeine emporia. At that point, the former CEO and founder of the company which took over the original single Seattle store and built it into a world wide empire, Howard Schulz, returned to his old job. No more than one month after this happened, one of us was in a local store in California, one of the 15,000 worldwide, and asked the manager if this had made any difference. "Oh yes", she said, "Communication is much better and we know a lot more about what is going to happen now. It's like night and day". We marveled at how this could happen, in one small store out of so many, and while we cannot attest to the effect on morale since we do not have (unfortunately) the contract to survey all the employees (we would accept coffee as payment), simply seeing the speed and magnitude of such a change was something to experience.*

---

* Although a good example of management change and its far-reaching effects, Starbucks is not immune to conditions during the financial crisis which rages as this book is being written. "£3 lattes" are a hard sell in an environment when so many are being laid off.

Identifying that management is the issue

In most cases this is not complicated. We stick with our philosophy that complex statistical tests of the data, arcane theories, etc. are not necessary to make such identifications. You will know when management is the issue when one or more of the following is found in your survey:

- In a question rating the skills and abilities of the manager the ratings of an individual are well below those of other managers in the organization.
- The overall morale of the group which is that manager's responsibility is significantly lower that that of other, similar groups or the organization average.
- The morale level for that manager's group has deteriorated since the last survey, both compared to itself and in relation to the organization as a whole.
- If the manager has a specific group of persons reporting to him (for example, scientists), and that group scores significantly lower in morale than other scientists in the organization.
- In the open-ended section of the survey, more than a few negative comments are made by more than one individual, about the management style or specific behaviors of that manager.
- Other factors external to the survey, such as turnover in that group, correlate with negative survey findings.[*]

One huge advantage of having the survey data is the ability to bring quantitative methods to something which is normally left to anecdotal ones. There is no denying the reality of the findings when the survey shows such big differences between one group and others, or deterioration over time. Any amount of defensiveness (and there will be a lot!) can be countered with this data.

Of course there are caveats:

- If the manager is new to the job and is coming into a "poor morale" situation, she bears little responsibility for what happened before

---

[*] This is not always the case since the survey results are a **leading indicator** and turnover may not yet have picked up. But in our experience the negative sentiment will surely be having an effect which will eventually have such a consequence.

and may not yet be known well enough for employees to form a judgement. The "negative halo effect" of previous management may hang over her for a while.

■ If there are external situations *specific to that group* which explain the poor results (for example loss of a big customer through no fault of their own, recent layoffs, etc.) the situation can hardly be laid at the manager's feet. As always, intelligent, as opposed to knee-jerk, interpretation of the data is called for.

What is the ideal "high morale" manager?

Our examples above might leave the impression that an "upgrade" always involves a change in personnel, and that is often true. But it does not have to be that way. What if it is possible to create, through training and other experiences, a manager who leaves behind a trail of goodwill and enthusiastic employees, no matter where she goes? What traits would this person have?

■ She would have left behind that part of her personal background and baggage which would have poisoned relationships with her team and her peers.
■ She would check her ego at the door and make sure it didn't effect her management style:
  – for example by not "stealing" credit for projects from others.
  – by knowing that when people in her team are successful she too is successful, not diminished.
  – by hiring or promoting people who might be smarter than her in the field and not being threatened by that.
■ She would have a view of people as essentially motivated, intelligent and creative.
■ She would believe that those qualities can be "invited" into the work environment with the right kind of management support and encouragement.
■ She would see her job mainly as a coach, not a controller.
■ She would have a profound respect for her people and treat them that way.
■ She would treat people with equality and fairness, not favoring some at the expense of others based on personal relationships, or other factors not related to the job itself.

- She would base all measurement processes of her employees on mutually-agreed-upon, clear goals.
- She would provide *honest, supportive, regular and timely* feedback to her people.
- She would be tough enough to make difficult personnel decisions, such as helping a low performing employee to face up to that fact.
- She would be a communicator of the stated values of the organization as well as living them via her own behavior.
- She would not tolerate violations of those values by anyone and would protect her team from those who would violate them.

If this sounds like superwoman, it is not: great managers do a lot of these things by instinct, but some of them can be learned. Others (like the essential ability to identify and control one's ego) can be a long-term personal growth project on which many do not wish to embark, and which is unlikely to change on a week-long course in the country.

So in a situation where management is clearly identified as the issue, the question then becomes whether a management change to someone closer to our wish list of "high morale traits" requires a totally new person or a "refurbished" existing one.

Change to a new manager or train the current one?

Organizations which wish to have high morale should not approach this issue as a "witch hunt" where they fire managers as soon as the survey results come out. That will poison the survey process and make it a source of fear, certainly in the management ranks, but also among line employees. Redemption must be possible, unless this is a repeat offender! If the individual has a track record of creating a poor morale environment wherever he goes (which some do) then firing is something which should have happened long ago and will be welcome with relief in that part of the organization which had the most recent displeasure of his management "style".

For other, non-recidivists, if management is identified via a survey as the core problem, can that person change? All around the world there are various training programs based on that premise, some internal to the organization, some external, which attempt to teach the "people skills" which a manager needs to create the high morale

146

organization. But is this something which can be taught? It comes down to this question:

Is a good manager born or made?

Our philosophy and that of many writers on this subject is that there is something of both nature and nurture in the "high morale manager". Some people, with absolutely no training at all, seem to hit the ground running from their very first management job. Their employees love them, even follow them to different organizations or jobs in the same one because it is so much fun to work for them. There is just "something about them", more than likely an alignment of the nature and nurture stars which has given them the traits we mention above. We would argue that they probably had grown up being given the same kind of respect which they now give to their people at work, but this is not always so. Even people who have had terrible child-hoods, but have worked through the later consequences of them, find ways to learn from the experience and vow to make sure that such an experience is not imposed on others. That is what therapy is for, and there seem to be no shortage of people wishing to pay for and make this journey. Others, though, remain unconscious of what they have been through, see themselves as quite "norm"al (sadly this is often true, they are the norm because there are a lot of unconscious people in our world), and they see no reason why they should change. Even if their behavior at home and in the workplace has the effect of a train wreck! But with luck, an organization will have at its disposal some great managers who have the happy coincidence of events which leads to "people friendly" skills and behavior.* Their survey results should reflect this, and barring unusual events outside of their control, usually do.

For those who fall short though, decisions must be made, and if the decision is to try and help that person improve, there must be an intervention of sorts. In terms of the action taken by the organization,

---

* We cannot emphasize enough that "people friendly", while sounding very "soft" to some is often something which is "harder" that it sounds. A "people friendly" manager will not allow one member of the team to undermine the productivity and high morale of the team and may have to deal very strongly with that individual. The word "friendly" here means "for the team", but not for everyone under all circumstances.

some are told "shape up or else", and are shipped off to a form of management boot camp which we found had limited value:[3]

> At the time of our study, this type of intervention was quite common, often conducted by facilitators with limited psychological knowledge or training, and could be so intense that the government (UK) was concerned that psychological damage could result. Our finding was that, while there was no lasting psychological damage, little real positive change resulted; since these were groups which were formed from people coming from many different organizations, we concluded that the short-term positive effects dissipated once the managers returned to their respective workplaces. We recommended that if such programs were to be effective, they should involve whole work teams rather than disparate individuals brought together for a week.

Others are prodded to go into internal or external management training programs of a less confrontational type, or given access to coaching staff who can work with them on a one-on-one basis. In terms of how managers react to all of this, we can divide people into those who wish to be lead to the water and are willing to drink, those who will reluctantly allow themselves to be led to the water but will not drink and cannot be forced to and those who don't think they need to go to the water at all. Those who have studied and worked in management training groups, as we have, have met all three types many times.

If we are to summarize our experience with "upgrading by changing personnel" or "upgrading by training and other forms of intervention", we must admit that many of our clients have had a high level of impatience with the length of time and investment necessary to "turn someone around" and choose to bring someone else into the job. That impatience is increased by the knowledge that a team is being damaged every day that that person is in charge, and that simply cannot continue. It is reinforced by the results we have shared with you: dramatic changes in morale when a new person is brought into the job. This is simply too tempting for them to ignore, and the choice becomes easy to make. Many of them argue, and it's a good argument, that their desire to "put people first" means they should and will protect the group at the expense of the one who is let go.

Management hiring and promotions as key morale factors

How many organizations look honestly into the areas of hiring and promotion of managers and consider the major consequences these have on the culture and morale of the organization? These actions have a huge effect, but it seems to us that so many times the decisions are made quite quickly, without such consideration. Yet the payback is often long-term and negative when a "people unfriendly" manager is placed in charge of a group: lowered productivity, perhaps lower customer satisfaction, turnover of the best people first, employee stress translating into health issues, knock-on effects at home, the list goes on. Surely the effort to make this more important (as some of our clients have done) is worth the investment. We believe it is, and we feel these are some steps which can be considered:

- Psychological testing and interviewing of candidates for the job. An experienced practitioner can tell the organization if this person is right for the job, would share the organization's stated values and culture, and would support a high level of morale. Of course there is no 100 percent guarantee, but the chances are greatly increased.
- More intensive and broader interviewing: we have read that Google's interviews for almost any job are said to be very extensive, certainly including group sessions with the team which this person is being hired or promoted to lead. Why not give team members such an opportunity? Their daily work life might hinge on this choice. Maybe this is a major contributory factor to Google being named each year in the top 5 "Best Places to Work" in the United States by Fortune Magazine?

Leadership will have to take account of the fact that, in so many organizations and perhaps their own, managers are hired or promoted into that role simply because they are technically skilled in the field they are managing. Ford Motor Company currently has a CEO who came from Boeing. His only connection with automobiles until he worked with Ford was in driving one to work at Boeing and previous jobs each day. Does that mean he cannot work successfully managing Ford? So far, even in extremely difficult times for the industry, he is doing extraordinarily well. While some skill may be important in the area being managed, in many cases it is not.

What some organizations forget is that managers are paid more not just because they might know more about the area they are managing than others. They are paid more because they have to manage people, and *managing people is a totally and completely different job than being a technical expert in that field, as anyone who has done it can attest.*

Goals and the manager's morale responsibility

Not so long ago, almost no manager we encountered had the management of morale as part of their goals. That has changed in the best run organizations: incorporating morale measures into a manager's goals is an intelligent step which creates a real focus for that person. Here is where *having a single-number morale index is essential and indeed is one of its huge benefits.*

The process involves the following steps:

- In the survey itself, identify items on which management has direct or indirect influence. Indirect might mean that the manager might not be responsible for developing a specific program, but certainly has responsibility for communicating it with her group. This question list becomes the basis for the "morale index" in your organization. Our experience was that nearly all items can be included, with notable exceptions which we covered in Chapter 2. It is also better in terms of management goals: if this were based on one or two questions, the manager might focus on only those two areas to the detriment of all others and the general well-being of the team.
- Have your internal or external specialists calculate the index at the completion of the survey process.
- Communicate the index results (the "score" for morale) to all managers and also to employees, for all groups more than 8 people. Sometimes there is nothing like transparency to motivate people.
- Incorporate the score into the manager's goals: performance below the organization average score might be incorporated as a goal to reach the average at the time of the next survey. There is also the chance to "raise the bar" for all managers, meaning that for those already at average, or above, improvements are still expected. The below-average-group manager therefore has to work especially hard

at this moving target, to make up the difference from before plus reach the newly raised bar; but this is as it should be.

■ Look for signs that the managers are taking advantage of this goal to learn more about morale and its importance, use internal or external resources to better their understanding, and making it as important as it should be. Perhaps it will not surprise people to know that our experience shows managers who become enthused and successful participants in this process as having the fastest track upward in the best organizations.

Management and morale: Consequences

The fact that management has the most impact on morale means that the consequences here are the most profound and our coverage here the most extensive of any step one can take. The positive payback from change is the greatest, and often the fastest, as in the Starbucks example above. At the same time, the damage caused by a bad promotion or hiring can be equally significant.

While we see this as the first place to look for changes, it is by no means the only action one can take to improve morale. Below we cover some of the other most important action areas which can have significant impact.

Step 7. Making changes: Flattening the organization structure

Having just covered management, we now talk about a method which eliminates it! This is not as strange as it sounds, it is simply another option, and a very powerful one at that. Restructuring to flatten the organization has some huge benefits:

■ Removing organizational layers reduces costs due to less management requirements; even entire central support functions can be cut.
■ It improves communication because each layer acts as a "sponge", first simply by being in the chain of information flow and secondly by the very human need to "justify one's existence".
■ By having less management to direct and control their activities, team members are freed and "empowered" to make more decisions

on their own, both individually and as a group. Since control and morale are highly correlated,* this alone can improve group morale.

One flattening strategy: Self-directed work teams

When combined with a concept such as SDWT (Self Directed Work Teams), the team takes over all that management once did and therefore avoids the morale problems created by managers whose people skills are less than adequate and which we documented in detail above. Peer pressure and group dynamics manage the group and deal with things that might have happened under a more controlled regime, such as favoritism by the manager, unfair reviews, ego problems, etc. This is not to say that groups cannot have problems of their own which might affect morale, because they can. But the group is in charge of dealing with them internally and in many cases, they seem to succeed. One common poster child of SWDT is the US steel company Nucor, which has used them extensively and very successfully.

Step 8. Making changes: Creating more equality

There are several ways that inequality manifests in the organization, and employees over the years have told us that these factors can have a major effect on morale. Let's look at an example we experienced.

A client company which was in the service industry, competing with some services supplied by the public sector, was in the process of taking itself public in an initial public offering (IPO). Part of the company's strategy during this time was to drive wages down to levels which would increase profitability and impress the money managers who would be targeted for investments at the time of the IPO. This resulted in a big gap between the public sector employee wages and those of this company, for the same types of jobs.

---

* Witness the fact that senior management morale is usually (but not always!) the best, followed by the next level of management and so on "down" the organization. This is usually explained by the factor of greater or lesser control of the work environment.

Around this time the CEO, in anticipation of a big payoff from the IPO, bought himself a brand new and high end Porsche, which he proceeded to park in his reserved spot directly in front of the corporate HQ. Employees walked past this everyday, including many whose wages had been squeezed down to impress the financial community. Many comments were received in the surveys about this and we recommended changes which would at least reduce this blatant demonstration of inequality in the organization.

Our example by no means implies that we believe in a flat compensation structure for all employees! But it does uncover more than one area of inequality:

- The *difference* between the compensation of the average employee and the top ranks.
- The "perks" which the top ranks receive such as special parking places (as an example, General Motors executives had a direct lift down to "heated garages" at Detroit HQ[4]), "executive dining rooms", etc.

Surely one can forgive many employees the wry smile or perhaps derisive laughter which greets company communications that on occasion say or imply "we're all in this together"? This is especially true in the United States, where the following statistic is true for 2009:

The average CEO pay is 300–400 times the pay of the average employee in their organization.

As far as we know there is no other country in the world where this is true. In Germany or France it is closer to 15–20 times. Were it 400, there would be an uprising which would put 1789 to shame. Imagine the "Storming of the Bourse"? Culturally, these countries would not allow it, and have put into law safeguards against it happening: the French do not have *egalité* in their famous *tripartite motto* for no reason.

This has been combined with mandated employee participation even at the Board level, such as in Germany. Any red-blooded US CEO will tell you that this is "socialism", but perhaps with a little less fervor since the historic, massive bailout of Wall Street in 2008–9! A bailout begun by a conservative Republican government, no less.

There are two ways to look at this:

- On the one hand, perhaps having such high-paid, top management in the United States motivates employees to try and move into that position themselves.
- On the other hand, the pay gap is a clear sign that "we aren't all in this together" no matter what the company tries to communicate to its workforce.

How does this come about? One of us having worked for two years in the salt mines of human resource consulting, compensation (including executive compensation), can speak with a little experience. It happens because of these reasons:

- US Board of Directors tend to be stacked with individuals who serve at the pleasure of the CEO. This also happens in the United Kingdom. In turn the CEO may serve on their Boards if they themselves are CEOs at other organizations. Turning down outright requests or subtle pressure from such a patron can be difficult. Having a "compensation committee" may not help change this, since this is simply a subset of the Board.
- Compensation consultants' checks are often signed or at least approved by the CEO. Again the pressure can be subtle, given such a connection. No outright demands need to be made: the consultant knows on which side her bread is buttered, and no matter how ethical or honest or independent she feels herself to be, the pressure to do the best for the client is there.
- CEOs constantly look at "what the other guy is making". With government filings, and business magazine features detailing such things every year, this information is widely available. This sets off an arms race to the top, with new and improved esoteric features, usually also tax friendly, always being added.
- The Anglo-American business culture supports a laissez-faire capitalism (until recently!) which means there are often no limits as to what is demanded and received by top management. Often this is justified by the fact that they have "added shareholder value". But there is a curious twist here: when they destroy such value, no penalty is paid. Indeed a "golden handshake" is often given even in the most egregious cases, where market share, profits and stock price are all way down. The Wall Street meltdown of 2008–9 has

provided what may turn out to be classic examples of what we are talking about, with the bankruptcy of Lehman Brothers, the 158-year old New York investment banking firm: as the ship was starting to sink, just before the bankruptcy declaration, Lehman gave multi-million dollar bonuses to several executives.[5] Not to be outdone, Merrill Lynch, about to be chomped up by the jaws of giant Bank of America, paid $3,600,000,000 (that is not a typing error) in bonuses right before the deal closed. Merrill then reported a $15 billion **quarterly** loss and the new combined entity asked for and received a government bailout![6] The question had to be asked, *"$4 billion in bonuses for a $15 billion loss, isn't that a little … er … generous?"* Our final example is General Motors (GM): when President Obama sacked the CEO late in March 2009,[7] he had presided over a 96 percent drop in shareholder "value" during his tenure in the top position;[8] for this he was rewarded with $23 million as a severance package!* [9] Needless to say the patience of US taxpayers was wearing thin at that point.

We are spending some time here because it is important. We see the opinions of employees on this subject and they get angry, often rightly so. The good news is that the 2008–9 financial market crash has exposed the dark underside especially of US-UK capitalism, and a new pro-regulation climate generated by the crash will undoubtedly bring in changes in this area.

Hopefully the new regulatory fervor will be balanced with some restraint, such that excesses will be removed while still allowing for the capitalist urges of entrepreneurs and others to exist. Some organizations have not waited for this, however, and have done some balancing of their own: to their credit, they decided some time ago that such behavior would not be tolerated and that they will take a stand on executive compensation. The best-known of these is the organic grocery emporium Whole Foods Market, Inc. (WFMI), which has stores in the United Kingdom as well as the United States. John Mackey, CEO, decided to set a limit ratio of 8:1 between any executive at WFMI and the pay of the average employee. WFMI is known for its

---

* As Fortune Magazine pointed out on May 11, 2009, the former CEO, Rick Wagoner, may not receive much of this sum if GM goes into bankruptcy, something which is widely expected to happen. Most of his $20 million plus "golden parachute" is in an annuity which is an unsecured obligation of GM.

good service and friendly, helpful employees, and we cannot say for sure that Mackey's gesture is the driving force in this. No doubt, though, that it is one of the morale drivers in the organization, since we have confirmed this as a result of numerous casual conversations with staff in the company.

As far as other "perks" are concerned, is it really *really* necessary to have "executive dining rooms" or "special parking"? Why not make the close-in parking available to all for some kind of recognition program, instead of for people who already have a lot of privileges?

This topic is so important that we feel the need to state that:

Failure to rein in the tendencies toward greed by top management, especially in the United States where this is most prevalent, **will undermine the morale and therefore the competitiveness of the workforce in that country**. At the same time, taking this unique current opportunity to create greater equality will be a major step forward; this could combine with technological and productivity edges in the United States and other major Western democracies, and will allow them to compete with emerging giants such as China and India in the decades ahead. Morale may become their only real competitive edge, but a distinctly powerful one.

Step 9 Making changes: Compensation practices

External Competitiveness and Internal Equity

The issue of fairness and equality has necessarily focused on executive compensation, but there is a whole world of regular employee compensation which has an impact on morale. Questions in any good survey will look at the three main issues here:

- Whether the employee believes that he/she is compensated competitively compared to the external world, *for the same type of job.*
- Whether the employee believes he/she is compensated fairly compared to others in the same organization, or so-called "*internal equity*".

- What the employee feels about any pay for performance programs (individual or group) which may exist in the organization.

One of the most fascinating aspects of having survey questions on this subject is the fact that one can test "reality" against "perception". In no other area of the survey is this usually possible, unless specific benefits are measured in the same way. Normally a survey is assumed to measure reality when enough people see something the same way. In our early example of the *ambush survey*, we mentioned that generalization from a data point of one was a serious methodological error. But a whole team saying that things are terrible is another story altogether!

In compensation, many organizations use consultants to provide data or buy into market surveys of salaries or wages of employees similar to their own. In this way they can see what a "Web Designer" is paid in the Midlands area of the United Kingdom, or a "Mortgage Loan Officer" in the south of France or Bavaria. Typically, organizations try to stay in a range of competitiveness which will allow them to attract and retain the talent they need. Some might even set their target at a higher level, say to be in the top 25 percent of payers for a given type or "size" of job.

But what if the organization finds itself very competitive in the actual marketplace and the employees come back in the survey and say they are "underpaid", compared to the competition? The gap between perception and reality is *one of communication*: they are unaware of the true value of their jobs in the market. This can happen for two reasons:

- They have an inflated view of what others make for that type of job, perhaps through faulty information they see or hear through the grapevine.
- They have an inflated internal evaluation of the "size" of their job and compare it to other jobs of greater complexity or responsibility.

To avoid the deterioration in morale which this perception could bring about, it is important to correct it via improved communication with the affected people. If the organization uses a job evaluation methodology like the Hay System, it needs to better explain how this works and why it is actually helpful to employees by being "incumbent neutral".* If there is no system in place, it will be important to demonstrate to employees the methodologies used to set salary and wage levels, share some of the market data which are used for this purpose, etc. Our experience is that this will counter any misinformation employees may have.

Survey data tell us that most people rate their pay in the "neutral" range, neither especially good or bad. This is to be expected, and should not be misinterpreted: few organizations can afford to pay under market in most advanced countries, or they will find themselves employee-free. On the other hand, they will not pay too much over market unless they have a death wish or a superb competitive position or a monopoly. While a figure of about 25 percent of employees will say they are underpaid (not usually backed up by market data), few, if any, will admit to being overpaid! Human nature seems to render such a self-perception impossible, for the hardworking and talented souls which we all are.

Pay for performance, anyone?

Speaking of human nature, the same impulse which makes most of us assume that we are at the very best slightly underpaid, also assumes that we are above average in terms of performance. Since this is, by definition, impossible (it makes one tail of the bell curve larger than the center piece, making it somewhat camel-shaped), managers have a problem going into an annual performance review even before one word has been spoken. Telling someone that they are "average" is seen as a terrible insult, and so clever organizational consultants have come

---

* The Hay System is delivered by the Hay Group, a worldwide consultancy with whom one of us was once employed. Like similar methodologies from other well-known consultants, the system measures the knowledge and problem-solving requirements, working conditions and responsibilities of each job, to generate a single number of "points". These in turn are used to compare the job to similar scoring jobs in the local/national marketplace and within the organization itself. "Incumbent neutrality" is achieved by measuring the job itself with the assumption of good performance, regardless of incumbent. As such the Hay System was an early and successful attempt to begin to break the "wage gap" between men and women, although by itself it could not change the eons-long and unfair practices in this area. Slowly, this is happening as women compete for jobs in every organization and the marketplace and cultural norms are forced to respond and open up.

up with euphemisms which might satisfy this human need while still meaning the same thing – *average*. This is why we have the phrase "meets expectations" and other crafty ways to avoid a yearly confrontation.

External competitiveness and internal equity are one issue but incentive or merit pay is something else again. As you might expect from reading this far, we have an opinion about what happens too often here. To illustrate how this opinion formed, let's look at a generic experience related to us in thousands on focus group interviews about the so-called pay for performance practice:

> Mary goes to the interview with her boss, designated as an "annual performance review". The review is over one month late but that is OK since last year it was two months late. She discusses her goals and whether she believes she reached them, which she does. Her boss generally agrees, which is certainly a good sign. She looks forward to receiving a good pay raise for the next year, based on this "exceeds expectations" evaluation. However, there is a problem: Mary has been working here for 10 years and has already reached the top of the "pay grade". Unfortunately, her boss explains, she will be limited to a 2.5 percent raise this year, as if she had only had an evaluation of "meets expectations". Mary leaves the meeting disgruntled, with much lowered personal morale. When she gets to her desk she begins the process of looking for a new job.

Whether it is because of a situation like this, one in which employee compensation is governed by a union contract, or a situation where a manager gives everyone an "above average" rating to avoid confrontation, there tends to be a vast homogenization of salary increases in so many organizations. When that happens, all possibility of increases serving their purpose of being "incentives" goes out the window, and morale is negatively affected. Why should someone work harder all year, only to be rewarded in exactly the same way as someone who does "just enough to get by"? We cannot think of any reason except the sheer joy of working in some jobs, and even there we guarantee you that most incumbents of even the most exciting jobs wish for some rewards which discriminate between poor and excellent performance. It is part of the need for recognition which we cover below.

We have seen the situation above so many times that we have a phrase with which we replace the usual "pay for performance" under these circumstances:

Pay for Pulse

The financial recognition for performance does not have to be at the individual level, of course. It is often difficult to parse out the exact part of a project which is attributable to one person versus another. Some jobs are easy to measure in terms of output, sales for example. Others are far more complex and have tentacles which reach into many areas. For these reasons many organizations have gone to group incentives. For Self-Directed Work Teams, group incentives are built into the very basic functioning of that entity: the team decides how this works and negotiates parameters with the organization as a whole. Only from your surveys will you find out what works best in your organization.

Step 10. Making changes: Recognition

Seemingly simple things do have larger-than-expected effects on morale. We humans have a need to be recognized for what we do at work. Some managers know this instinctively and find ways to do it on a regular basis. It is not time consuming or a great burden to let people know they have done a good job, or are appreciated in some way. It is simple and it raises morale. We know this because when we correlated individual questions with the overall score on morale, the one on recognition had one of the highest correlations (the question focuses on whether an employee's manager is seen giving him/her appropriate recognition for a job well done). For some the word "recognition" brings to mind special ceremonies in which employees are brought forward to be given some kind of gift along with praise from management for a job well done. This is certainly an occasional part of the process but it is far more than that; recognition is much more important as a *continuous process* whereby even small and seemingly insignificant events are noted and thanks exchanged. The "manager from hell" will never do this, he has certain attitudes which preclude it.

- The employee is paid, that's recognition enough!
- It's too time consuming!

160

- Doing the job is not something to be praised in any way, it's the minimum requirement for keeping it!
- (Usually unconsciously): I never got this at any time in my life, and therefore neither will you!

Management training programs cover recognition, for those who do not have it hard wired into their psyche. While the spontaneous and ongoing support of team members in this way is more natural and effective, it is better to do it in a way that is "learned" and more rote than not to do it at all. In spite of the fact that it is easy to learn, so many employees complained about the lack of this in our surveys and this can and does affect their morale. No expensive "programs" required.

MAINTAINING HIGH MORALE IN YOUR ORGANIZATION

Throughout this book we have stressed the importance of building a "high morale culture", and stressed that this approach is crucial to success in this area. We have done this because of the temptation among some organizations to treat morale as an occasional area of focus, perhaps when things are really bad, only to be ignored at other times when the financial tide comes in and all boats rise. Having a culture of high morale means that one is always vigilant and always ready to act to build and maintain something which is seen as so valuable, and delivering the benefits we have detailed throughout this book.

Any number of situations can and will have a negative effect on the morale level, and that will be only the beginning of an organization's challenges because, as we should recall:

Morale is a leading indicator

As such, it will give you an early warning that *worse is to come if you do not take action against a drop*. All the benefits which the organization is receiving can disappear, and all the things which morale prevents can return, if morale drops far enough: customer satisfaction and productivity will go down, employee absenteeism and turnover will rise, and that is just a start. Having up-to-date information is therefore critical.

Keys to morale maintenance: 1. Ongoing measurement

Although this might seem like a shameless push for the consulting profession, it is an easy decision for nearly all clients who take on the morale improvement process. Organizations which survey their employees nearly always commit to it on an ongoing basis: the average between-survey period is 12–18 months for a full census, but sample surveys can be taken much more frequently now with Internet technology. There is one caveat here: the potential for *"over surveying"*, or *"survey fatigue"*, whereby the recipients start to get bothered by the process if it is used too frequently; response rates can then go down. Surveys have become such a ubiquitous part of life now, that this is possible. At the same time, a glance at the Internet news sites during elections, for example, shows that there are still many people who will complete the online surveys offered. Again, response rates will be the key indicator as to whether the organization is going to the well too often. A simple question in the survey can also test frequency preferences.

The measurement process, properly carried out, will provide all the information you need to spot early trends and target action:

- Lower morale versus previous surveys, either overall or in specific groups.
- Lower morale following a management change.
- Lower morale following an HR policy or practice change, such as a new overall compensation system or salesforce reward protocol.
- Flat or lower morale in a specific group, in a year when the organization overall is trending upwards (divergence).

Keys to morale maintenance: 2. Quick, decisive action

A management change which results in a noticeable drop in morale is an easy one to reverse and yields quick results. Many other factors driving a negative change in morale can be identified by managers and teams from their data; often mitigation is a simple shift in practices based on team members' suggestions. We found this so many times: changes often cost very little yet make such a big difference. In the world of an office or a small factory, "little" things become big things. Placement of furniture, quality of equipment, availability of supplies, arcane practices held over from "the old days", all these can grate on employees and are so easy to change before they really start to effect morale.

The key is to listen. In organizations new to this process, even if only one thing is changed, it will be seen by some as a miracle, based on what they experienced before. "You mean, we actually have a voice? We can make a difference?" they will say. Quick action, **connected back to the survey or the focus group input**, is a reinforcement for the employees that there really is a connection between them sharing their opinions and change happening. This means power, it means control; and that translates into higher morale.

Keys to morale maintenance: 3. Effective communication with the workforce about morale

It is very important to remember that employees are intensely interested in morale results. If you have a survey and put a question in there which measures this, you will already be well aware of this fact. They want to know if their opinions are representative of others in their team, or in the whole organization. They want to know if their team is improving in morale, perhaps as a result of something they themselves did, such as a group training in which the whole team participated. If morale is going down, let them know that too. Don't believe for one minute that not saying something will mean that the employees don't know it anyway. If the manager of the team is the reason for that and you are sure of that fact, don't let that person do the feedback and take action to stop the decline.

In summary, open and honest feedback of results is critical here, and *will protect and enhance your investment in the morale measurement and improvement process*. Don't sugarcoat, and keep the level of openness high: your employees will appreciate it and in any case will see through any attempt at cover-up.

All this is important, but what about avoiding the possibility of facing low morale scores in the first place? Is advanced protection possible? Yes, if the organization is vigilant about avoiding the scourge of low morale: we call this the "morale killer".

Keys to morale maintenance: 4. Identifying and dealing with morale killers

Morale killers: Avoiding or reforming the "boss from hell"

A recent experience related to us by a friend brings one of our least favorite characters to life: the friend, a highly experienced and skilled individual who had worked in the financial services industry, was interviewing for a job. She had had children and badly wanted to return to the workforce. The interview went well, until she mentioned that she needed a little flexibility in order to be able to work around her childcare activities. The interview immediately went poorly and she left with the distinct impression of not wanting or indeed being offered the job. As she left, the interviewer's assistant whispered to her: *"Its just as well, he has had 52 people in that job in the last 5 years!"*

Our readers have become familiar with the "boss from hell" at this stage, and he is surely the dinosaur of all morale killers, which refuses to move swiftly toward extinction. Avoiding this beast means careful promotion and hiring practices along with training and other intervention activities; these might enable the organization to rescue the milder offenders from the terminal fate of their more fearsome brethren, to attempt to release the "kinder, gentler" creature inside them. But reform is not always possible and one must take action, especially at the management level, with those who cannot or will not allow themselves to be changed. This is easier when one adopts a philosophy and perspective like the following:

Morale killers: When all else fails, sacrifice the one for the many

This is going to sound harsh, but it is a truth which we have experienced over and over. If someone is standing in the way of the creation or maintenance of a high morale team through his behavior, and if he has been given a chance to "come around", *he must be sacrificed in the interest of the team*. It does not matter that he was great "back then", that he has been in the organization a long time, that he is the *technically* most skilled person in the field and so on. It matters that *here and now*, he is standing in the way of progress toward a high morale culture, with all the many benefits which flow from that situation. It matters that he does not embody the values which you say are at the core of what you do. For this reason our clients have always been advised to not be timid when it comes to such matters: wasting time for someone to come around means only that valuable team members will become disheartened, so much so that they might pull back on the job at the very least, or even leave. Replacing such team members will be time consuming and expensive, or if they have really deep and valuable knowledge, might even be almost impossible. The cost to the organization of such morale destroyers, especially when they are in positions of power and influence such as management, is enormous. Act soon and act decisively!

Morale killers: Health issues and stress

We have seen in the performance section of this book the extraordinary data which is being generated on the relationship between morale and factors in the workplace such as management and health issues. This should leave no doubt that employee heath is at risk when people are exposed to toxic individuals, especially those who have power over them. But what of the "generally known fact" that some jobs are more stressful, regardless of who is running the operation? We look on this with a degree of skepticism, and our own data has bolstered that view. For one thing, one person's stress is another's excitement and challenge; this means that *if you find the right person for the job*, there should be a match between its stress level and how the person manages, or even enjoys, that stress. Make the wrong choice and you have a morale-destroying situation, for sure.

Our Emergency Room example from Chapter 2 is also relevant here: on the one hand, a seemingly stressful work environment did have terrible morale in one hospital but an equally stressful one in another sister hospital beat every other department in the morale sweepstakes. With apparently equal "stress" as a common factor, one has diametrically opposed morale results. Of course, unless you just picked up this book and turned to this page, you will understand our basic morale philosophy well at this point, and this makes sense when based on that, *management makes the difference, not the external environment.*

Morale killers: Stop pretending, start doing

Too many organizations have top or mid-level management which reads all the right books, goes to all the right seminars, comes back and says all the right things, and yet, nothing really changes. Why is this? Because real change requires more than words, it often requires a shift inside the individual making it. In organizations, real change often involves letting go: of power especially, but also of prestige, of ownership and especially of ego, and many are simply afraid to do this. They do not want to "empower" anyone because they secretly love to control everything and are scared to death of letting that go. They do not want to give out too much information because that is one of their levers of control. They do not want to cut their organization for the sake of the whole because the size of their domain determines their (fragile) inner sense of worth.

Some of these people flat out refuse to change and they are easy to spot and manage. The ones we are talking about here are those who pretend to be moving in the right direction, but don't. Don't be fooled by this stealth species: the employee survey will identify who they are, that is one of its huge benefits. Make an ultimatum: walk the talk, or walk the plank!

CHAPTER 6

CURRENT TRENDS, ISSUES AND MYTHS IN EMPLOYEE MORALE

INTERNATIONAL TRENDS IN EMPLOYEE OPINIONS

One of the most interesting aspects of working in this field is to see how different groups of people respond to surveys measuring their morale. Being able to rank them and see the differences is something which certainly has captivated our clients over the years, as they looked at data from their organization and compared the performance of different units. But if we step back from a single organization or even industry, and look at some of the differences *between countries*, that truly can be an eye-opening experience. Having access to large international databases is the key here, and so we draw for this section on the valuable work done by the international human resource consultant Mercer.*

Ranking countries by morale

Mercer takes an approach to employee engagement which is different from some of the other large consulting firms we have talked about here. The data we will look at is drawn from their 130-item questionnaire, unlike other firms which use a small number of questions to

---

* Data and illustrations appear with permission of Mercer, are from January 2008 and available on their website at: http://www.mercer.com/pressrelease/details. htm?idContent=1292085#Ex1, along with extensive linked free content.

measure this factor. While we might call this a "morale" survey, Mercer uses the term "engagement" to refer to the overall measurement they generate from this large-scale survey questionnaire.

Looking at engagement across cultures in the chart below (Chart 11), we see that Mercer's current database of some large countries shows India well ahead of the pack. With a +25 percent score or 25 percentage points above average, India's performance is impressive, well ahead of its "BRIC" cohort of fast-growing economies, of which two others also appear on this chart (China and Brazil), while one does not (Russia). As a very general rule, a difference of 10 percentage points (different from ten percent) is statistically significant in most comparisons of one group with another, in this field of work. Is India's performance here to be expected? To a great extent, yes: when an economy emerges from a long period of relative stagnation, workers see boundless opportunity and have a strong emotional reaction to their new-found freedom to work, make money and reach the "middle class". This was also true in the 1990s after the fall of communism: Hungary, the Czech Republic, Poland and other newly liberated countries had huge leads on our international morale charts at that time.

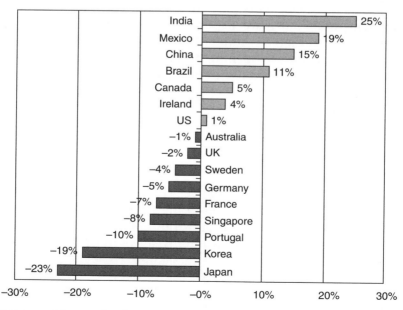

CHART 11   **Mercer database of engagement by country, percent favorable**

Also of great interest is the position of Japan and Korea, at the bottom of the chart; this was also true in our own data as long ago as the 1990s, while Japan struggled with its "lost decade" after the crash of its real estate bubble. Following that, Japan's corporate culture changed dramatically, abolishing lifetime job security; mass layoffs ensued. It seems from the Mercer data that this cultural shock wave may still be having an effect all these years later.

Looking at the chart, it seems that even with strong protections built into labor law in EU countries such as Germany, France and Portugal, whereby for example firings at will are not permitted, this does not translate into a high level of engagement. Perhaps contrary to expectations, even six-week (or more) vacations don't seem to help those who have them move up the engagement ladder. While Sweden has changed and lessened its famous cradle-to-grave social welfare programs, it still has an extremely generous offering for its workforce, but engagement does not follow automatically, as we see from the chart. In the free-wheeling, fire-at-will (in most states) Unites States, with its typical two-week vacations, and with the rather similar United Kingdom and Australia, engagement appears to be about average, but far better than that of their continental Europe cousins. How can this be? It is because, absent massive societal change as in Japan, morale is driven so much more by local factors such as interaction with management than by anything else. It can also happen that when employees receive such largesse as the long European vacations and bulletproof job security, it can create a sense of "entitlement" where expectations are significantly raised, which then filters everything at work through its lens. Things can then be seen as "lacking", which in other countries would be gratefully received. As we have discussed before, having such a sense of security is not always the best thing; a limited degree of fear is motivating, and a total lack can be a source of apathy for *some* workers.

Engagement drivers by country

As part of its international survey efforts in engagement, Mercer has extended its data-gathering to examining the *drivers of engagement* by country. They accomplish this by asking survey participants a question directly on this subject, rather than infer it from other question responses. The question listed the factors, in Table 6 below, and asked participants which one most affected their sense of engagement with their organization. This gives us a fascinating view into what workers are looking for in each culture. The table sets this out in detail:[*]

TABLE 6 **Mercer table of engagement factors by country**

	Global	China	France	Germany	India	Japan	UK	US
Respect	125	121	133	129	104	90	144	122
Type of work	112	75	138	113	116	107	122	112
Work-life balance	112	98	133	106	97	119	119	111
Provide good service to customers	108	108	110	108	103	79	122	107
Base pay	108	113	110	105	103	140	117	114
People you work with	107	96	105	131	98	107	120	104
Benefits	94	127	81	110	94	75	76	112
Long-term career potential	92	91	89	77	108	94	88	92
Learning and development	91	83	67	80	98	86	85	82
Flexible working	87	85	77	92	80	88	83	88
Promotion opportunities	85	92	79	83	113	92	68	80
Variable pay/bonus	80	111	77	65	86	123	56	75

Note: Scores near 100 are of middle importance, scores below 100 are less important, scores above 100 are more important.

If we take the first row, "Respect", we see that there are some major differences between different cultures. The UK workers place more than 50 percent more emphasis on this as an engagement factor than those in Japan. Interestingly, too, with "Respect" at first place overall, we see support for the argument that it is not labor law-based factors such as job security which drive engagement (and morale): it is much more *the emotional relationship they have with their organization*. This in turn is usually mediated by their supervisor.

---

[*] Data appears with permission of Mercer.

Some notable parts of this database are:

Benefits: As might be expected, Chinese employees rate this highly. In a country where the health system has moved from a socialized system to much more of a "pay as you go" (and often "pay in advance") one, it is understandable that employer-provided benefits would be so important. What is interesting, though, is that in Germany, with its comprehensive and high-quality, mandated health-insurance system, a significant emphasis is also placed on benefits.

Base and incentive/Bonus pay: Both base and variable pay such as bonuses are extremely important – more than any other engagement factor – to Japanese workers. Indeed their score of 140 on base pay is the *highest for any country on any factor*: Yet in India, where one might imagine that pay is still very much catching up to Western levels, it is not nearly as important for workers as the type of work they are doing and their promotional opportunities.

People you work with: Germans place more emphasis on this than anything else, closely followed by Respect. In China and India, the people aspect is not nearly so important, a big drop down from the German scores.

Providing good customer service: Japanese employees say that this is of much less importance to them than other countries' workers. Is this because the level of service, driven by a culture which insists on politeness and respect for customers, is already so high?

Work-life balance: French workers rate this very highly, as do Germans. All but Chinese and Indians seem to agree, but do not feel as strongly about this as the French. What implications does this have for the future competitiveness of Western industrial nations? It is interesting that two of the BRIC countries are saying that this is not an issue for them. Will they be working harder that the rest of us as we try to find that balance? Only time will tell whether their scores increase on this factor, along with their standard of living.

The Mercer data give us insight into some fascinating issues and show the differences that do exist between groups. They also demonstrate that an external database can be extremely valuable.

As Mercer states in the material accompanying this chart and table, it is possible to misinterpret employee survey data when one does not have the perspective of such data. This appears at first to be a powerful argument against our own caution of relying too much on such normative resources due to reliability questions! However, we believe a happy medium can be found between these two positions: having access to this type of data for general comparisons by country, etc., while at the same time using one's own data as the main internal norm, with all the benefits we described in Chapter 2.

Ethics and morale

This is a currently relevant topic to which a whole book could be dedicated. To illustrate, lets look at two hypothetical companies:

- ABC Bank participated intensely in the recent housing run-up and subsequent crash. It made loans to people who barely had a pulse, let alone a qualifying income or a steady job, because it knew that it would soon be selling these loans off to the securitization industry, which would slice and dice them and sell them to investors all over the world. In the mind of ABC's top executives, this was the ultimate in "spreading the risk". ABC knew that many house appraisals conducted as part of its loan origination process were wildly optimistic and out of line, but this did not matter too much to them because the market would "go up for ever". When ABC crashed, the CEO was paid his contracted severance of several million dollars; other executives joined firms which would feast on the coming foreclosure crisis, seeing this latest step in their career as just "going with the flow", and hardly stopping long enough to appreciate the irony of profiting from a situation which they had helped create. Thousands of ABC employees were laid off and had trouble finding any work at all.
- XYZ Bank spent the last few years doing what is does best: being a great organization which takes care of its customers and employees. Having these two strong relationships with key stakeholders helped it get through the severe economic downturn, and while XYZ revenues dipped somewhat, even at the worst point they had not gone down more than 10 percent. Still this was enough to depress cash flow, so XYZ went to its employees and asked them to cut their work hours and pay, also by 10 percent. All agreed, knowing that this would

mean no layoffs. XYZ had not participated in the subprime loan debacle nor had it traded in credit-default swaps. Throughout this time, XYZ continued to make the usual payments to the employee pension plan and did not cut benefits. Regular contributions amounting to 3 percent of profits to charities and special local events were maintained. As fuel costs rose, XYZ benefited significantly from its heavy investment 2 years ago in green electricity co-generation facilities for its large suburban HQ facility. This combined with power from the solar panels which covered all of its huge roof to supply nearly all the company's HQ energy needs. All branch banks had been instructed to contract with local utilities for use of as much sustainably generated power as possible. In spite of the economic downturn and the slightly higher cost, XYZ continued to fulfill its mission as a major recycler of its waste, both at HQ and in the branch offices. Its won awards for its Green efforts.

Which of these companies do you believe would have the higher morale? Would that morale have anything to do with the ethics and values of the companies? These might be the simplest questions we have posed in this book. With new generations coming into the workforce (see below) and the focus of those generations very much on ethics and values,[1] the environment, sustainability, green energy, etc., demands will be made on companies to become more environmentally friendly and ethically upstanding. These new workers will be consumers too and they will not want to work for, buy from or do business with ethically challenged or environmentally damaging dinosaurs. But before any organization rushes out and drafts an ethics statement and distributes it to all employees, fair warning: as *HR Magazine* reported in 2000, when such ethics statements are not lived, they actually drive down morale.[2]

TECHNOLOGY AND MORALE: THE TELECOMMUTING REVOLUTION

Inevitably, the forward march of technology is having its impact on workers' lives and therefore on morale. But the constant reach provided by communications technology with its smart phones, Wi-Fi and other broadband wireless networks linked with laptops having the full power of a portable office, has created a paradox: it means that many workers are tethered to their work as never before while at the same time being "liberated" from an office. The rationale for many office dwellers showing up everyday in a central location is being eroded, and organizations are finding that in return for investment in the technology which keeps everyone connected, real estate costs can come down dramatically. Why pay for a nice office in a shiny tower when Fred or Mary will gladly work at home or at a local coffee emporium? Will they work, though? Or will they end up distracted by family at home or be tempted to focus on things other than the company's business? The pace of change in the direction of telecommuting and the fact that companies such as IBM seem to be making this move so forcefully, suggests that means have been found to mitigate the possible negative effects suggested by this question, in order to benefit from the positive effects. It is important to bear in mind too that the suggestion that people will not work without constant supervision is a nod to the more primitive view of man which we described earlier on in the book: the one in which the worker has to be closely watched and coerced at all times to be productive. The success and amount of telecommuting seems to suggest that the more enlightened view of self-motivated workers is winning this argument. Having clear goals for which the individual can reach no matter where they are physically located every day, is likely a key to success here.

But how does all this affect morale? Is the at-home or roaming telecommuter more satisfied, happier to be "free", or does she miss the camaraderie, the chance to catch up in person, the chats around the coffee pot? There is a study which has examined this topic[3] whose findings are helpfully summarized in a press release[4] as follows:

Telecommuting is a win-win for employees and employers, resulting in higher morale and job satisfaction and lower employee stress and turnover. These were among the conclusions of psychologists who examined 20 years of research on flexible work arrangements.

The findings, based on a meta-analysis of 46 studies of telecommuting involving 12,833 employees ... "show that telecommuting has an overall beneficial effect because the arrangement provides employees with more control over how they do their work", said lead author Ravi S. Gajendran. "Autonomy is a major factor in worker satisfaction and this rings true in our analysis. We found that telecommuters reported more job satisfaction, less motivation to leave the company, less stress, improved work-family balance, and higher performance ratings by supervisors."

With one small exception (workers away from the office three days or more per week reporting a worsening in their relationships with co-workers), evidence such as this study points to a positive outcome for telecommuting, which drives a higher level of morale while lowering costs in many cases. This convergence of benefits will doubtless increase its use.

GENERATIONAL ISSUES AND MORALE

When the Baby Boomers* gave way to Generations X and Y, there were sure to be seismic shifts in the workplace of those countries where this occurred. Of particular interest in the study of morale is the Y generation, because of their reputation as the "Trophy Kids",[5] young people who expected and received a reward in a sporting event simply for taking part, regardless of result. It also seems to be the case that "grade creep" could be a contributing factor; this is where students received grades for work which were higher than those received by previous generations, adjusted for quality or performance. London's *Daily Telegraph* reported a few years ago that fully 86 percent of University students in the United Kingdom were expecting to graduate in one of the two coveted top grades; some 60 percent did, which is significantly higher than earlier generations' achievements.[6] While there is some truth to the old circular joke that all generalizations are wrong, the implication of the Trophy Kids' expectation of bountiful rewards being transferred to the workplace would be negative for morale: they would expect praise at every stage, and rewards for simply showing up. Not receiving these would lower their personal satisfaction and morale, make them less engaged; this in turn could try even the most patient manager. In this case, the generalization might just have been right: HR departments are reported as having some problems with this cohort[7] and special training programs have been devised to help cross-generational communication within the organization.

---

* Baby Boomers: 1946–61, although an inexact estimate as are all generational time frames; Generation X, 1961–81; Generation Y, 1976–2001. Source: www.wikipedia.org.

With morale in mind, this sounds valuable. At the same time, it is comical to think that entire organizations must bend to the whims of a new generation whose sense of entitlement is perhaps somewhat "out of whack". This attitude will come face-to-face with the fact that as other groups such as the Boomers retire, Gen Y workers will take their place, often being asked to do more with less, which hardly sounds as "rewarding" as their expectations. Fortunately, Generation Y is far from being a one-issue group: they appear to be very multicultural, are open to change and self-reliance.[8] They will have their challenges, as all generations do, but hopefully their sense of entitlement will be tempered by life experience and they will use their many positive attributes to contribute richly to the fabric of morale where they work.

MORALE AND TIME ON THE JOB: THE "MIDDLE" YEARS

If you plot employee survey data with morale on one axis and time on the job on the other, and you have enough data, you will find something rather discouraging: a significant drop in morale from the early years on the job, like we see below in Chart 12.

What does this tell us? Quite simply that there are two times when we are really *really* happy on the job:

1. *Right when we are hired and for a short period thereafter.*
2. *Right before we retire!*

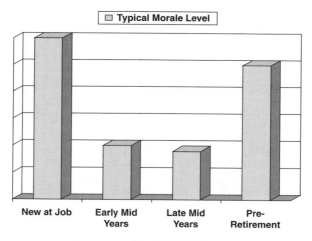

CHART 12   The "middle" years

The rest of the time we slip down in to the "middle years", comfortable perhaps but not nearly as enthusiastic, engaged or whatever you wish to call it. For this reason many organizations go to extensive lengths to mitigate this effect. The concept of *job enrichment* partly came out of this need to bolster morale and performance in the middle years. Moving people across jobs to stimulate them, or if that is not possible, improving their current job, these are strategies which have been successfully used to counter what seems to be a worldwide trend. Of course some might say that in these challenging times with thousands chasing after few jobs at a time, no job enrichment is needed, but this is shortsighted. You do not want a large section of the workforce disengaged in this way, the productivity and performance losses will be significant and your organization will pay the price for them. In addition to the two actions above, any time you can give more decision-making authority to such people, remove unnecessary blocks to their creative contribution to the organization's success, you are working effectively against this trend and pushing the U curve upward from its dip.

WORKING FOR THE FAMILY BUSINESS

A lot of organizations say "we're all family here" but what if most of the employees ARE really "all family"? How do you fire your son ... or your father? How does a matriarch/CEO not show favoritism between her children who also work at the family firm? What if her personal relationship clouds her perception of the performance of her children? Does she go easy on them, even if they perform badly, because she is their mother? If so, how does that affect the morale of non-family employees? How do you give notice to quit to your Dad and disappoint him to his core? What if the "boss from hell" *is* your Dad? Can you confront him even though you have a huge desire to please him and be just the son he wants you to be? How can family feuds be kept from the workplace when family *is* the workplace? That is usually the one place where one can escape from such things.

Clearly, the family business raises a lot of morale questions. What implications does a family relationship have for morale? We have worked for family companies and there is a cultural uniqueness about them which can be very enjoyable. It can also be difficult, as our examples demonstrate. We have no data which shows whether family-owned and operated businesses have higher or lower morale than those which are not (that would be an interesting study), but we are sure of one thing: family involvement is a unique challenge. Nepotism is always possible there, with far stronger potential than in non-family owned and operated businesses. Sticking to principles of good management regardless of family ties would be good advice but terribly difficult to implement. How many times have we seen sons or daughters of the patriarch placed in top positions, who then fail to achieve the results expected of them? That is when it becomes clear, yet again, that family membership and the right name are not qualifications for effective leadership of any significant organization. Then the family, perhaps very reluctantly, reaches to the outside for help, and the family member goes off to do what he or she really wanted all along, perhaps far from the family business.

DEBUNKING TEN MORALE MYTHS WITH SURVEY DATA

One of the most enjoyable and profitable exercises one can accomplish with morale survey results is to debunk what are generally accepted "truths" about the organization in general, its stated core values or its human resource practices. It is not that we experience *Schadenfreude* when doing so, it is simply that shining light where it is not often done can be quiet "illuminating" at times and can lead to real change. This is not to say that it might not ruffle some feathers of those whose ego is invested in the status quo! It is also enjoyable to rebut some myths which grow up around the *employee morale process* itself.

Myth 1: Guiding principles, core beliefs and stated values are often really "lived" by the organization

This is one of the easiest areas to test with survey data. By simply looking through an organization's mission or values statement and creating questions in the survey which list these, one can ask if they are in fact true. We have seen so many cases where they are not really "lived" that we have lost count. This can be quite a demoralizing set of data for top management, at least for a while; but when an organization does this *it no longer has the illusion* that what it states is actually the experience of its employees. Then comes the sometimes humbling

178

but valuable task of admitting that this is fact and beginning to really live the stated values. Employees will, in our experience, appreciate the honesty which is involved in this, compared to the charade with which they lived before.

Myth 2: Morale is driven by staffing levels or activity levels ("busyness") of staff

This can also be easily tested. Simply correlate a morale index with the staffing data and one has the answer. We had the opportunity to do this with a large hospital system:

We often heard statements from departmental managers in this organization about "full time equivalent" employee (FTE) levels and census (hospital occupancy) numbers. Most frequently, the argument was made that low staffing levels were contributing to low morale, and/or that a high census was making employees too "busy" and thus having the same effect. Sometimes, the opposite argument is made, i.e., that low census is increasing employee anxiety levels and lowering morale. Was this true? Or was it another example of the blame game?

To find out, we went back to our database of hospital employee surveys completed for a large, for-profit system in an eighteen month period. While we had surveyed many of these more than once in that period, only one set of data was included, that of the most recent survey. In all, we had data from some 77 hospitals across the country (US), comprising about 25,000 employees. All major geographic areas were represented, and all hospitals used the same survey instrument. At the end of the survey process, we collected data from our client as to census levels, FTEs per adjusted occupied bed and patient satisfaction for each hospital, *at the time of the survey.*

Using our proprietary software, RCI/In*Sight, we analyzed the data to produce a rank order of morale in each hospital and across all hospitals. In other words, each hospital was compared to all other hospitals combined. The first question we wanted to answer with this data was whether FTE numbers affected morale: the answer is not at all. In other words, if we knew the number of FTEs per adjusted occupied bed at any given hospital, it was impossible to predict with any accuracy how morale will turn out in that unit.

We then examined the relationship between census and morale: while there was a slight downward trend line, indicating that morale did go down slightly as census went up, this relationship was statistically insignificant and census therefore gave us no predictive ability for morale scores.

We know from this data therefore that neither staffing levels nor census appear to be related to morale, at least in this example. But before we leave these two areas, we need to answer another question, usually one that comes in a "Yes, but ..." format after the previous sets of data have been shared. For example: "Yes, but don't the hospitals with less employees suffer from lower patient satisfaction, even though they may not have low morale?" To answer this question, we plotted FTE levels as before but in relation to the patient satisfaction data that had been collected for each hospital by an independent survey company, during the period of the employee survey. We found no connection between FTE levels and patient satisfaction, at least not in our nationwide 77-hospital sample.

The second "Yes, but ..." questions usually sound like this: "Yes, but don't hospitals with a high census and very busy employees have lower patent satisfaction, even though they might not have low morale?"

This hypothesis, while appearing to have logical face value, did not hold up. We found no relationship between hospitals with higher census and patient satisfaction, nor vice-versa.

Whether or not these findings hold up in your organization is something we encourage you to discover. We know that, in the case of this client, management had some valuable data with which to counter "generally held beliefs", beliefs which were the source of frequent complaints from some employee sources, but which turned out to have no basis in fact.

Myth 3: Pay is a leading driver of morale

Although this is a counter-intuitive position to take, we place less emphasis on pay as a driver of morale than some others in our field tend to do. The main reason is that some powerful experiences have molded our opinions on this subject. For example, during a period some time ago, one of us was working for a large service organization which operated around the world. This organization instituted a new pay policy for new employees in order to save money: they would be paid at about half the level of longer tenured workers, especially at the beginning of their careers. The idea was that, eventually, the lower paid workers would catch up with the higher.

We were in a position to observe some workers on the job while this was happening and saw the situation with our own eyes. We spoke with customers of the company, who knew of the new pay scale, and who were without exception, sympathetic to the "plight" of the new workers, and the fact that they had to work side by side with their high paid brethren. We then had the opportunity to survey all employees to see how things were really going. The results were astounding but in retrospect, perhaps very understandable: *the lower paid staff had far higher morale than the higher paid*. This meant something very important to the company: the more they expanded in this way, the higher their average morale would become! But why and how could this come about? First of all, the newer employees were young, a major correlate of higher morale compared to middle-aged workers, as we saw above. They were glad to have jobs, the economy had been somewhat difficult for a while and these jobs had good benefits and "perks". Secondly, they had no perspective of how things were back in the "good old days", when pay was high and working conditions easier. Their perspective was decidedly in the present, which freed them from the complaining of their older co-workers. The third and equally important factor is that pay is overrated as a morale driver. It is not one of the major factors which workers look for in a job, except in some countries (see earlier in this Chapter); it is also clear that in industrial countries and under most economic scenarios, an organization must pay competitively just to get someone in the door. This means pay is automatically "OK", perhaps not great, but certainly the market rate for the job.

For these reasons, we are skeptical of those who say that this is *the* all-important factor at work. It is not.

Myth 4: Job security is a major factor in morale

Much has been written about job security as a basic need of workers before there is any chance of a good morale level in the organization. We agree with this, but only up to a point: one way to look at this is to ask employees, in a survey, what they look for in a job. The list of desired items on the question can be quite long, citing things such as good pay and benefits, challenge, a chance to learn new things, a chance to be around interesting people and, of course, job security. Here is what we found.

*In most organizations, except those in monopoly situations or in heavily regulated quasi-public sector or actual public sector entities, **job security was nowhere near the top of the list of desired attributes in a job.***

The question then becomes, why do books on morale often state that it is such a key element? We believe the main reason is that there is a threshold, below which it becomes very important, but above which it is not. To illustrate this we turn to the old joke that when you give a drink of water to a man lost in the Sahara, the next thing he wants is theater tickets! Translated into the workplace, if a basic level of job security is established and large-scale firings or layoffs are quite unusual, most people forget about job security.

A second element comes into this and that is individual differences: from our studies, we find organizations where:

- Job security is high
- But it is also highly desired by the workforce

The conclusion from this is straightforward: people congregate in jobs which provide them with that they want, what a surprise! People looking for job security might congregate in the public sector, where layoffs are rare and strong union protection ensures that no random act of management can threaten them. Or they might go to jobs which are in monopoly positions such as power companies, where demand for their service is steady and predictable, and fluctuations in financial markets or in technology cannot threaten their security. The only problem with this is when changes in regulation occur, when public sector moves to private for example, as during the Thatcher years in the United Kingdom. Suddenly, people who have signed up for something which matches their needs find themselves in a whole new world. Of course some thrive, but we saw evidence that many do not, they pine for the "good old days" and in the worst cases quietly retire on the job. Being launched into a competitive world after being a monopoly provider can be quite shocking but also exhilarating to those who grab the challenge.

Many people will recognize this, having been through or watched the EU-ordered privatizations in France, Germany, the United Kingdom and even the Greek telephone company OTE (which seemed to hang on to its state-owned status for a long time before capitulating, much like the airline Alitalia). In the Unites States, with less history of state-owned industries (until the recent bailout created one of the biggest purchases in history, much to the chagrin of many Americans!), these types of changes occurred with deregulation. Power, telephone and airline companies woke up to dramatically new landscapes which their cultures were poorly prepared to face, and a Darwinian process ensued. Many disappeared because they were ill prepared, and were gobbled up by those who had done the work.

There is also an element of workers who are so secure in their own skills and abilities, that even a relatively insecure organization would not bother them: they are safe in their position and know they can always find work somewhere. They also tend to be more flexible geographically, and usually younger. This flexibility and confidence in their employability empowers them and makes them much less vulnerable to being "victimized" by circumstances. Our readers might be surprised how many such people there are in certain areas.

Even if they are not a member of such a group of supremely confident individuals, a certain segment of the workforce (and it is a much bigger segment that its opposite), does not list job security at anywhere near the top of their wish list for a job. Technology workers will always list "a chance to learn new skills", "a chance to do challenging and interesting work" in the top three. Job security might make it into the top 7 items, or it might be even lower.

We call the process of finding the job which fits ones hopes and fears and values *"self-selection"*.

Some might say that its all very well to dismiss job security in flush times; but what about when unemployment is much higher, or layoffs have already occurred? How does that affect morale? Again it all depends on expectations: to illustrate this, look at Japan in the 1990s:

During the so-called lost decade, Japan suffered a devastating bursting of asset values (such as real estate), which had spiraled out of control to such an extent that the real estate value of the land under the Emperor's Palace and grounds in Tokyo was worth more than all the real estate in California. Using the equity built up from such an explosion, Japanese investors bought properties at inflated prices around the world. When the bubble burst it not only took Japanese prices down, it crushed a cherished part of Japanese culture which had been in place for a long time: guaranteed lifetime job security. Our surveys of Japanese employees at the time showed that the results were devastating also to morale, with Japan scoring some of the lowest scores in the world.

With the expectation of job security built into the culture, taking it away is a terrible blow. The extent it is built in varies by culture, however. While far less than Japan, Europe has a higher expectation of job security than the free-wheeling, "fire-at-will" United States, and has incorporated it into EU and local laws which protect workers much more than that received by US workers. This has a downside though: French, Italian and other companies we spoke to over the last 15 years expressed some frustration at the impossibility of firing someone who was clearly not pulling their weight, and cited the effect on morale of having a "free loader" in a team who benefits from team productivity while contributing little. Why should this person receive an equal share of the team bonus? This view receives some sympathy from us; we see a balance as optimal, with some worker protection being necessary, but matched with protection for the organization in terms of being able to redress the "freeloader" situation.

So far we have talked about what employees want; but another issue here is that many organizations simply do not want people working for them whose main desired attribute in a job is job security. A technology company on the cutting edge wants people who are willing to take risks and explore new ways of doing things. Does an employee whose main concern is her own job security fit this profile? Not likely, her motivation will be one of protecting herself and her job. So not only do most workers say that job security is not #1 for them, but many organizations say they want other values to come first in their workforce.

Research study: Job security does not generally drive morale:

Except in extreme cases, where for example job cuts have been announced but not yet enacted, or our Japan example above, morale is not driven to any significant degree by feelings of job security or lack thereof. If morale were entirely dependent on workers' sense of job security, those with the most security would be happy employees indeed. On the other hand, those whose job security is tentative at best and whose continued employment depends not just on the possession of a detectable pulse at year end, but only on how they perform day to day, (for example, entrepreneurs, commissioned sales people and many others), would be a miserable bunch. Even a cursory glance over one's daily contacts with people in these different types of jobs would indicate that both these hypotheses are completely insupportable. To back up this assertion, lets take a look at more of the employee survey data we collected among 25,000 employees in 77 hospitals (many of which had undergone some form of downsizing, due to pressures in the industry). Our data showed that if we knew how employees responded to a simple question on job security, where they were asked to rate that factor at their hospital compared to other hospitals they knew, and we plotted that response against overall morale, the chart had a "shotgun" look and the *relationship yielded a correlation close to zero. In other words, knowing the job security ratings would give us **no** predictive power as to the overall morale in a given hospital.* But can responses on any individual question provide that kind of predictive power? In the same study, we found that knowing how employees perceive *management ability* gave us a good idea as to how overall morale would turn out. This appears to be a far more potent factor in determining morale than job security, and has been borne out in studies outside the healthcare industry.

Myth 5: Layoffs are an effective management tool

Some research findings

The basis of much job insecurity is the threat of layoffs, "downsizing" as it is euphemistically called, or even the somewhat grotesque "rightsizing". Such activity is at epidemic levels in the United States and to a lesser extent in Europe as this book is being written and the financial crisis is unfolding. Even in this difficult context however, some organizations are finding ways to do things differently: they are asking employees to take lower wages or to work less, in order to save jobs. It stands to reason that only an engaged workforce would let that happen, one which already feels like a team and which would take it for granted that the group helps the individual and vice-versa. Such an action would never be attempted in a low-morale environment, because it would never work. If the underlying philosophy has always been "dog eat dog", then that is exactly what you get in times of economic stress.

Regional culture also plays an important role in whether layoffs are used or not. As a recent newspaper article pointed out,[9] Taiwanese employers, faced with rapidly falling orders for their electronics products such as semiconductors, are bending over backwards not to lay off workers. The report states that as of March 2009 some 100,000 of 130,000 workers at Hsinchu Science Park are being asked to take unpaid time off, even to the point of that being 10 work days per month. "Solidarity" carries quite a cost for these people, as the article points out, but one which cultural norms make bearable. Such activity is almost unheard of in the United States.

The question remains however, if layoffs are used, do they work? Or are they desperate measures for which there is a long-term negative price to be paid? We will use external research to examine this and the issue of the "layoff survivor", and then use some of our own research on survivors and job security, which adds to our case for lessening the focus on job security as a key factor in morale:

Bain and Company research on layoffs[10]

This international consulting firm looked at US layoffs during the difficult period of 2001–02 after the "dot com" bubble burst. Many of these layoffs were in the telecommunications industry. Bain found that there were certain myths about "downsizing" which their research debunked, specifically:

- *Even in such a severe downturn,* **most firms (70%+) did not resort to layoffs.**
- *Those companies which did lay off workers during this period saw their share prices* **rise less, or fall more**, *than those which did not. Stock markets do not like layoffs, investors often interpret them negatively for the organizations concerned.*
- *Layoffs can be dangerous to* **management's** *health: in the week after firing someone, managers' chances of a heart attack* **double.**[11]
- *Expected paybacks for layoffs often* **fail to materialize.**

Institute of Behavioral Science study of layoffs[12]

In this study of one large US company with between 80,000 and 100,000 employees in the particular division which was studied, researchers attempted to show that layoffs had an effect on employee health among the "survivors". The latter group was broken into those who might have known of downsizing in the company but had no contact with it, those who had moderate contact with the process and those who, while not being directly laid off themselves, had a great deal of contact with those who were let go and saw the process in action.

The company seems to be what the researchers call a "chronic downsizer", which is the last thing one would ever recommend to a client, dragging the process out over years. On top of this, the actual numbers of those let go were staggering: some 27 percent of the workforce in 1997 (with another 13 percent warned of possible layoff but not actually being laid off at that time) followed by another 20,000 in 1999. A "few thousand" were hired back in between. Doing the calculation based on the higher total number of original employees reported, it would appear that up to *half the workforce* had been let go during the course of this study.

As one might expect with these numbers, the extent of the layoff process and long drawn out time line had its effect: *the closer an employee was to what had happened, the more there were health and worker injury problems. The group which reported "no contact" with the layoff process or any of the employees being "downsized", fared best.*

While these findings are interesting, we would not generalize them to all organizations which perform layoffs: for one thing, this is a sample of one company, with a chronic habit of laying people off, and huge layoff percentages. This chronic practice never gives survivors a chance to feel the relief that would go along with thinking "its over and I am still here!" None of this is typical. There were also some methodological issues to which the researchers readily admit: all health matters were self-reported as opposed to being collected from clinical records, and the factor of depression was seen as mediating (coming between and perhaps driving) the layoff process and some of the health issues. This means that those having the worst health issues after seeing a layoff in their organization may be those who are already suffering from some level of depression. Did the depression therefore "cause" the health issues or did the layoff experience? If both, what percentages are attributable to each? An even more intriguing question for future research might be: Do depressed workers sometimes get laid off before others, due to the effect of the depression on the quality of their work?

While we have no doubt that layoffs can be extremely painful for workers to whom this happens, and even those who survive, we also want to add some of our own research to this issue, as we explore another myth.

Myth 6: Layoffs *always* drive down morale of survivors

While we have seen that layoffs are often a very ineffective way to manage any business, let alone the damage they do to peoples' lives, they sometimes *have* to happen for the organization to survive. Do they always lead to lower morale? That is certainly the assumption, but is it true? A study we did of the electric utility industry some years back may shed some light: using surveys of 100,000 employees in that industry, we divided the 30 surveyed companies into those that had had some significant job cuts in the previous 18 months and those that had not. *There was no difference in overall morale between the two groups.* How can this be explained, especially in the light of what we have just studied? As surprising as this may sound, it makes some sense. We believe this reflects the more normal situation of a once-off layoff, where the positive "survivor" effect can occur. As long as more cuts are not expected and even though employees are often asked to do more with less, they are still around and have survived to work another year, or much longer. It is interesting that this industry, electric generation, transmission and delivery, often attracts people who score higher on "job security" as a desired factor on the job that those in other industries. If layoffs affect these people so little, they are likely to have much less effect on those who value security far less.

Myth 7: There are only small differences in morale between groups

For some reason which we cannot fathom, some writers refer to the "fact" that big differences between morale within organizational groups or across geographies do not exist. This is not true! Just looking at the data with which we started this chapter, we see the huge differences between Mercer's morale database in India versus Korea or Japan. In your organization, provided it is not very small, there are such differences. If you are not seeing them, it is because you are either not looking, or not looking with the *right tools*.

A ranking system which gives you a composite look at "how we are doing" is *essential* to any morale measurement process. Once it is in place, you will be able to compare groups with each other and see the magnitude of the differences, and perhaps not be so surprised at what you find. Be sure to take every opportunity to look at the demographic breakouts such as age, time on the job and sex, for example. Many times we have been able to talk to clients about major issues which they have, which we discovered from these often hidden aspects of the survey data. If 80 percent of the women in your organization say that promotion practices are not fair, watch out! You have not only a potential legal problem but an actual or future management and morale one too.

Myth 8: If you don't measure it, it doesn't exist!

This is one of our personal favorites, also known as the "head in the sand" or "let sleeping dogs lie" method of management. We did not make it up; this has been observed in the trenches of the consulting world many times. What is surprising is that even well educated and experienced managers and executives can use it, when it is so patently absurd. The idea is that by not surveying, for example, whatever is "out there" will not exist. This is familiar to students of philosophy as the argument that when the tree falls in the forest and no one observes it, it did not happen. Unfortunately, this is not some lonely forest, it is your organization, and even if it is not measured we can assure you it does and will continue to exist! Of course, the very fact that someone would make this argument is a good sign that there really is something bad out there; all the more reason to go in and see what it is.

Myth 9: Smaller organizations are higher in morale than big ones

The argument here is simple: small means that everyone is accessible, there is no "remote" management issuing edicts from on high. Managing by walking around is possible for "top management" on a regular basis, no long distance train or airplane rides necessary. And all of this adds up to high morale. There is only one problem: as we saw from the Hilti data, it was not true there. The scattergram showed a shotgun effect and almost zero correlation between the Hilti units' size and

189

their morale; this happened in a company where the individual units really do differ significantly in size from one country to the next.

If you are not yet convinced, we took the 2008 data from *Fortune* (US) Magazine's annual "100 Best Places to Work For" feature (already featured in Chapter 3) and correlated the rank order of the 100 organizations in that list with two items: size in terms of employee levels, and growth in jobs. *Size correlated 0.1689 with rank order*, meaning that as the organization got smaller there was a slight tendency to be higher (lower number rank) on the list, but this was *not a statistically significant result*. (Growth in jobs was a negative but insignificant correlation). *The 2009 data was similar.*

Our thesis remains intact: management makes the difference, not the size of the organization. Even in very large organizations, high morale is a possibility, as much so as anywhere else.

Myth 10: "Morale" is dead and "engagement" has replaced it

We saved this one for our last myth because it brings us full circle to something we briefly covered when defining morale in Chapter 1: the issue of management trends and "must have" items, whereby something becomes fashionable for a while and threatens to wipe out the "old way" of doing things. Consider the following argument from Professor John Eldred, co-founder of The Wharton School Family Business Program in a *BusinessWeek* article from 2008.[13] He states in that interview that he does not like the world morale, finds it "paternalistic" and the idea that it can be improved "arrogant". In its place Eldred has a prescription which, he believes, will fill the gap, a focus on "spirit, engagement, and energy". He states that in a high-energy environment, workers can help themselves instead of just waiting for management to help them.

The main problem with this is, as we have seen before, semantic. This is like saying, *"intelligence is an outdated concept, an arrogant attempt to measure complex factors within the human mind; we should focus instead on **mental acuity**!"* In a clever entry in his blog, technology HR consultant Steven Cerri takes Eldred's argument apart by using the examples Eldred puts forward for improving "engagement" and showing that each one is in fact a tried and true morale booster![14]

Our discussion of morale and engagement in Chapter 2 showed that, for all intents and purposes, many are using these terms in the same way, believing that they are quite different. While some like Gallup use new and extensively researched questionnaires to capture engagement, some other organizations' questionnaires which used to measure morale are now used to measure "engagement", *with few changes*. Where there has been some parsing and separating the meaning of engagement from that of morale, it is mainly in the academic world, but that behavior has not moved into organizational life; there, only words have changed. Eldred is also misguided when he believes that "energy" alone is enough to help workers achieve their goals. This is easily debunked by looking at any number of organizations which have lots of "energy" but no real direction, or lots of energy expressed in dysfunctional ways.

It seems to us that a sensible way of dealing with this is to have "peaceful coexistence". Engagement has created excitement among some practitioners and users of their services, and that is a good thing. It is also easy to say employees are "engaged" (as we do many times in this book), and morale does not lend itself to such easy one-word use ("moraled"?). Creating a well designed "engagement index" from overall, general morale data, is valuable. But to suggest that this is a breakthrough with the impact of the printing press (we admit to exaggerating somewhat for effect) is a bit much.

So, morale is alive and well, it still packs the power it always has, in fact more so; and many thoughtful consultants like Cerri would agree with this.

CHAPTER 7

EMPLOYEE MORALE AS A RESPONSE TO CHALLENGING TIMES

Early on in this book we asked you if you knew how your Beijing employees were doing. Perhaps it is fitting therefore that we come full circle to China to begin our closing comments. More than the structure of this book drives this, however, the twenty-first century will be, there is no doubt, the Chinese century. How we compete and cooperate with this emerging giant will shape all our economies, and the world stage. As we were researching the possibility of using the famous Chinese word "wēijī", or crisis (see above), we were chastened and amused by an article written by a China expert, Victor H. Mair, professor of Chinese language and literature at the University of Pennsylvania.[1] As Professor Mair tells us, the widely disseminated idea that this word means both "crisis" and "opportunity" is completely misguided: instead it holds the meaning of "danger with uncertain outcome", nothing as optimistic as some Western interpretations. Professor Mair's advice is timely: as we write this book, the largest economy in the world is in crisis and at a crossroads and other major economies are teetering. "Danger with uncertain outcome" is everywhere and optimism might even be seen as foolhardy. The fear level is palpable.

No doubt, out of this crisis will come change, something which the US voters chose in President Obama and will receive, maybe in greater quantities than they ever imagined. The phrase "better be careful what you ask for, you may get it" comes to mind. US car companies are on life support and one or even two may go bankrupt, major investment banks which had survived the Great Depression have disappeared, household names such as Merrill Lynch have been swallowed up and unemployment is rising to record levels.

Given that the United States is an engine which drives much of the world's economy (while that is changing, such change will not happen overnight), its sub-prime-driven melt-down is affecting other economies around the world, particularly one which is often seen as parallel to the United States in corporate culture, the United Kingdom. It is interesting that while the US situation was the driver of things to happen later, the first sign of real crisis came not from the United States but from the run on the bank Northern Rock in the United Kingdom, which belied its name in spectacular fashion. That had not happened in the United Kingdom *for more than a century*.[2] China may be rising, but it is not immune: with its vast export business to the U.S., its factories at home are idled by lack of US demand, and its domestic demand is nowhere near developed enough to make up the slack. Indicators of distress are everywhere and rising: in Italy, shoplifting of food (especially parmesan cheese) is at high levels by first time offenders, often middle class; the French are doing the unthinkable and ignoring "sell by" dates on grocery items.[3] In this interdependent world, all are hurting.

This is a humbling experience for many people in the business community; as the financial version of the "100-year flood", none will have experienced it before or will again. But when all is crashing around us, when government is the "bank of last resort" and is being resorted to daily, is it the right time to be thinking beyond the crisis to a time when mere financial survival is no longer at stake? Is it the right time to ask questions like "what have we learned?" and "is there a better way of doing things?" We think it is the right time, which is why we referenced it in the title of this book. Vulnerability always makes for more openness, it cracks the defenses that have been used to protect and shore up the "old ways": witness the changes people make in their lives after a divorce. Well, part of the divorce this time, we hope, is from some of the management practices which have been exposed by the crisis. As the famed investor Warren Buffet is widely quoted as saying, "when the tide goes out, you get to see who has been swimming naked". In this case we see whole companies which were naked, literally: the world's largest insurer AIG had few, if any, assets backing hundreds of billions of dollars in esoteric insurance contracts they had written. Also figuratively naked were the CEOs and other management of many of these companies, who had for decades enriched themselves while building a house of cards. Perhaps Buffet had "naked greed" in mind when he made his now celebrated statement; more than anything else, this seems to be the image which we will take away from this fiasco.

We don't see many of the companies we have lauded in this book in the *"hall of shame"* list of fallen companies over the last two years. Only one, which we would not put in the hall because of the overall good treatment of its workforce, has had a layoff.* The others were too busy leveraging their superior levels of morale to survive the crisis, like Hilti doing whatever it took to *not* lay off people. Instead there were taking the necessary steps, mindful of employee interests at all times, to make their way forward. They will benefit when things get better, which they will. Perhaps others will look at them and say, *"well that really worked for them during an unprecedented downturn, maybe it would work for us too"*. The answer is that it would work well. Consider this: *if it works now, with the need to just survive, imagine what high morale would do in "normal times"*.

Since we clearly cannot depend on the goodwill of some of the captains of industry to "do the right thing", more regulation is in our future, something which the London G20 meeting of political leaders emphasized; but can we regulate ourselves into a better future? To be sure, more regulation is necessary, but it too holds danger with uncertain outcome: overreaching, overmanaging by government will kill the goose which lays the golden eggs. There is no longer any doubt that capitalism is the driving force for prosperity and a high standard

---

* While we were writing this book, Starbucks closed 991 stores worldwide in two stages and laid off thousands of employees. With stores on opposite street corners in many cities, they had over-expanded and were cannibalizing themselves. This came into harsh highlight when the deep recession hit. Aside from this, we stand by their positive management practices as an example for others and expect them to rebound as the economy improves.

of living for so many: China itself is a de facto capitalist economy and is benefiting enormously from that fact. But capitalism is also the driving force for incredible greed and out-of-control risk.* Finding the happy regulatory medium between freedom and control will be difficult.

A goal of high morale fits well into this scenario. It is a strategy of potentially great competitive advantage. As we have demonstrated, morale has so many benefits it is hard to imagine why all organisations do not make this a number one priority. This goal is timely: into the window of opportunity opened by the exposing of capitalism's dark side, comes the chance for many organisations to redirect their energies. Especially in the US., but not only there, greed can be replaced by a more equal way of doing things. Is there any reason why US corporations' CEOs should walk away from years of failure with a handsome payout, when a fired worker who fails gets nothing? As we have shown, America likes to think it leads the world in everything, but that is not true in morale: its actual and emerging competition is way ahead and that will prove to be a compelling advantage if the gap is not closed. Improving morale is one of the most economical, most efficient, most powerful ways to change an organisation: the winners in this twenty-first century will know and exploit this by making management practices which drive it higher, their top priority.

If we seem to be picking on the United States, let us expand our review: the United Kingdom also does not score especially high on morale. It shows itself to be reluctant to bring in high performance management practices which would drive its scores higher, and often stays with traditional "top-down" ways of doing things. This will bode poorly for relationships between management and workers in the future and for its competitiveness worldwide. France, Germany and Italy, from the Mercer data and our own, do not seem to be benefiting from long vacations, rock solid job security and other legally mandated aspects of the work environment. It seems that their 6-week vacations become "the minimum expectation", not something extraordinary in the context of work life around the world; and with

---

* We are not suggesting that capitalism is unique in these attributes: as George Orwell so astutely pointed out in *Animal Farm* (1945), communism created a cynical system, like for the pigs on his farm, where everyone was equal but "some were more equal than others".

this expectation comes a sense of entitlement, not higher morale. But at least there, one has a different social contract which does indeed contain a crucial element of higher morale, if only matched in other areas of management practices. We are talking about a sense of fairness and at least some equality; not equality for all jobs and all people, but a leveling of the playing field between *different and equally important stakeholders* such as management and the workforce.

When this message is shared in the United States, it is often met with some resistance, but the recent election shows that it has lessened: Barack Obama – with his message of a more equal society, clearly spelled out to the voting public, of health care for all instead of some, reining in of executive excess, tax cuts for middle income Americans and not the rich – won a decisive victory in the polls. Americans are ready and willing to try something which would have been unpalatable a few years back, and that something includes *a more egalitarian society*. This bodes well for practices which can and will improve morale: imagine workers who could never get health care, being able to cover their families. Imagine them knowing that they are sharing a little more of the pie, not having to listen to someone making 400 times what they do telling them in videotaped messages that "we're all in this together". What if all this happens not as a result of heavy-handed regulation, but because of a shift, albeit small, in the shared values and sense of common good? Is this a case of "back to the future"? It should be remembered that early states such as Massachusetts, Pennsylvania, Virginia and Kentucky called themselves a *"commonwealth"* in their constitutions, and still do. Perhaps America is ready to get over its unease with at least some more government intervention in daily life and some sharing of the "common wealth"; this makes sense anyway, given the reality that the government already provides more than half the health care in the country via "Medicare" (age 65 and up), extensive coverage for the poor ("Medicaid") and the Veteran's Administration (for the military). It is also a reality that as the lender of last resort, the United States would have collapsed without the historic government intervention we have recently seen and "life as they know it" would have disappeared. These are hard facts to swallow for some, but might bode well for a different future of morale in the world's largest economy.

No matter for what reason and what resistance it meets, it is a shift which is needed, and we have tried to demonstrate why: morale is a key driver of performance. Absent from this book are long lists of what to do on Monday morning to improve morale, although we certainly did not ignore this issue. Instead we chose to focus much more on performance in order to push the debate, every so slightly, in that direction. It is something we believe is critical, and a message we take everywhere we go. An example is on one of our websites, where we point out, in relation to well-being/morale, that *"getting psychological well-being right is at the heart of being a successful organisation"*.[4]

Around the world, organisations will be looking for competitive advantage as the economy becomes more "globalized". Morale provides this without the need to outsource, lay off workers or bring in a new "boss from hell" who can drive the workers harder (for a while, until they leave). Its time has come, and if we do things right, "crisis with uncertain outcome" can indeed become opportunity.

NOTES

WHAT IS MORALE?

1. American Psychological Association (APA): morale. (n.d.). WordNet® 3.0; accessed August 27, 2008, from Dictionary.com website: http://dictionary. reference.com/browse/morale.
2. American Psychological Association (APA): morale. (n.d.). The American Heritage® Dictionary of the English Language, Fourth Edition; accessed on August 27, 2008, from Dictionary.com website: http://dictionary. reference.com/browse/morale.
3. http://govleaders.org/gallup_article_getting_personal.htm, accessed on June 12, 2009.
4. Frederick Winslow Taylor, *The Principles of Scientific Management*, Harper & Brothers, 1919.
5. Douglas McGregor and Joel Cutcher-Gershenfeld, *The Human Side of Enterprise*. Contributor Joel Cutcher-Gershenfeld. Annotated, illustrated edition, McGraw-Hill Professional, 2006.
6. Terrence E. Deal and Allan A. Kennedy, *Corporate Cultures: The Rites and Rituals of Corporate Life*. Contributor Allan A. Kennedy, p. 4. Revised edition. Da Capo Press, 2000.
7. Marvin Bower, *The Will to Manage*, New York, McGraw Hill, 1966 (original source of Deal and Kennedy quote above).

HOW DO ORGANIZATIONS MEASURE MORALE?

1. "Job Review in 140 Keystrokes", BusinessWeek, March 23 and 30, McGraw Hill, 2009.
2. Likert, Rensis (1932). "A Technique for the Measurement of Attitudes". *Archives of Psychology* **140**: 1–55.
3. David Sirota et al., *The Enthusiastic Employee*, Appendix D, Wharton School Publishing, 2005, pp. 321–3.
4. http://en.wikipedia.org/wiki/Employee_engagement; no publication cited; accessed on October 27, 2008.

WHY MORALE IS SO IMPORTANT

1. Jeffrey Pfeffer, *The Human Equation: Building Profits by Putting People First*, Harvard Business School Press, 1998, p. 138.
2. Terrence E. Deal and Allan A. Kennedy, *Corporate Cultures: The Rites and Rituals of Corporate Life*, Allan A. Kennedy, contributor, revised edition, Da Capo Press, 2000, p. 4.
3. Marvin Bower, *The Will to Manage*, New York, McGraw Hill, 1966 (original source of the Deal and Kennedy quote).
4. Terrence E. Deal and Allan A. Kennedy, *Corporate Cultures*, p. 5.
5. James R. Evans and Eric P. Jack, "Validating Key Linkages in the Baldrige Performance Excellence Model", reprinted with permission from *Quality Management Journal*, April 2003, vol. 10, no. 2, © American Society for Quality. No further distribution allowed without permission.
6. R. S. Kaplan and D. P. Norton, "The Balanced Scorecard – Measures that Drive Performance", *Harvard Business Review* (January/February 1992): pp. 71–9.
7. R. S. Kaplan and D. P. Norton, *The Balanced Scorecard*, Boston: Harvard Business School Press, 1996.
8. James R. Evans and Eric P. Jack, "Validating Key Linkages in the Baldrige Performance Excellence Model". Reprinted with permission from *Quality Management Journal*, April 2003, vol. 10, no. 2. © American Society for Quality. No further distribution allowed without permission.
9. http://www.gallup.com/consulting/52/Employee-Engagement.aspx
10. David Sirota et al. *The Enthusiastic Employee*, Wharton School Publishing, 2005, Chapter 2, pp. 33–53.
11. Sirota Survey Intelligence press release, April 5, 2005: http://www.sirota.com/pressrelease/MoraleStockPrice405.pdf
12. http://www.extensor.co.uk/articles/int_levering/interview_robert_levering.html
13. Doug Jensen, Tom McMullen and Mel Stark, *The Manager's Guide to Rewards: What You Need to Know to Get the Best for – and from – Your Employees*, AMACOM Div American Mgmt Assn, 2006.
14. http://www.haygroup.com/ww/Press/Details.aspx?ID=1361
15. David H. Maister, "Practice What You Preach: What Managers Must Do to Create a High Achievement Culture", Free Press, 2001.
16. Ibid., p. 9.
17. Jeffrey Pfeffer, *The Human Equation: Building Profits by Putting People First*, Harvard Business School Press, 1998, p. 138.
18. Ibid., Chapter 2.
19. Ibid., Chapter 2.
20. Barry A. Macy and Hiroaki Izumi, "Organizational Change, Design and Work Innovation: A Meta-Analysis of 131 North American Field Studies, 1961–1991", in W. A. Passmore and R. W. Woodman, eds., *Research and Organizational Change and Development*, vol. 7, Greenwich, CT: JAI Press, 1993, pp. 235–313.

21. James R. Evans and Eric P. Jack, "Validating Key Linkages in the Baldrige Performance Excellence Model", reprinted with permission from *Quality Management Journal*, April 2003, vol. 10, no. 2. © American Society for Quality. No further distribution allowed without permission.

22. Milé Terziovski and Danny Samson, "The Link Between Total Quality Management Practice and Organizational Performance", *International Journal of Quality & Reliability Management*, 1999; vol. 16; issue: 3; pp. 226–37

23. C. Ostroff, "The Relationship Between Satisfaction, Attitudes and Performance: An Organizational Level Analysis", *Journal of Applied Psychology*, 1992, 77, pp. 963–74.

24. Ibid., p. 965.

25. Edward E. Lawler, Susan Albers Mohrman and Gerald E. Ledford, *Strategies for High Performance Organizations: The CEO Report: Employee Involvement, TQM, and Reengineering Programs in Fortune 1000 Corporations*, Jossey-Bass Publishers, 1998.

26. Benjamin Schneider, Paul J. Hanges, D. Brent Smith and Amy Nicole Salvaggio, "Which Comes First: Employee Attitudes or Organizational Financial and Market Performance?" *Journal of Applied Psychology*, 2003, vol. 88, no. 5, pp. 836–51.

27. Ibid., p. 836.

28. Daniel R. Denison, *Corporate Culture and Organizational Effectiveness*, Wiley, 1990.

29. James K. Harter, Frank L. Schmidt and Theodore L. Hayes, "Business-Unit-Level Relationship Between Employee Satisfaction, Employee Engagement, and Business Outcomes: A Meta-Analysis", *Journal of Applied Psychology*, 2002, vol. 87, no. 2, pp. 268–79.

30. Ibid., p. 274.

31. F. J. Landy, *Psychology of Work Behavior*, Pacific Grove, CA: Brooks/Cole, 1989.

32. Timothy A. Judge, Carl J. Thoresen, Joyce E. Bono and Gregory G. Patton, "The Job Satisfaction-Job Performance Relationship: A Qualitative and Quantitative Review", in *Psychological Bulletin*, 2001, vol. 127, no. 3, pp. 376–407.

33. M. T. Iaffaldano and P. M. Muchinsky, "Job Satisfaction and Job Performance: A Meta-Analysis", *Psychological Bulletin*, 1985, vol. 97, no. 2, pp. 251–73.

34. Timothy A. Judge, Carl J. Thoresen, Joyce E. Bono and Gregory G. Patton, "The Job Satisfaction-Job Performance Relationship", p. 387.

35. M. Roznowski and C. Hulin, "The Scientific Merit of Valid Measures of General Constructs with Special Reference to Job Satisfaction and Job Withdrawal", in C. J Cranny, P. C. Smith and E. F. Stone, eds., *Job Satisfaction*, New York, Lexington Books, 1992, pp. 123–63.

36. "When Service Means Survival", *BusinessWeek*, 2 March 2009.

37. Mark Graham Brown, *Keeping Score: Using the Right Metrics to Drive World-Class Performance*, AMACOM Div American Mgmt Assn, 1996, p. 177.

38. Geoff Tennant, *Six Sigma: SPC and TQM in Manufacturing and Services*, Gower Publishing, Ltd., 2001, p. 9.

39. Mark Graham Brown, *Baldrige Award Winning Quality: How to Interpret the Baldrige Criteria for Performance Excellence*, Productivity Press, 2007, pp. 53–4.
40. E. Anderson, C. Fornell and S. Mazvancheryl, "Customer Satisfaction and Shareholder Value", *Journal of Marketing*, October 2004, 68 (4), pp. 172–85. Retrieved November 26, 2008 from Business Source Complete database. Reprinted with permission from the *Journal of Marketing*, published by the American Marketing Association.
41. Ibid., pp. 12–13.
42. Sachin Gupta, Edward McLaughlin and Miguel Gomez, "Guest Satisfaction and Restaurant Performance", *Cornell Hotel & Restaurant Administration Quarterly*, August 2007, vol. 48, pp. 284–98;analysis of restaurant management.
43. Available online at www.kenblanchard.com. Registration may be required for certain research articles.
44. Jack W. Wiley and Scott M. Brooks, "The High Performance Organizational Climate", in Neal M. Ashkanasy, Celeste Wilderom and Mark F. Peterson, *Handbook of Organizational Culture & Climate*, SAGE, 2000, pp. 177–92.
45. Kenneth Bernhardt, Naveen Donthu and Pam Kennet, "A Longitudinal Analysis of Satisfaction and Profitability", *Journal of Business Research*, February 2000, vol. 47, issue 2, pp. 161–71.
46. Wiley and Scott, "The High Performance Organizational Climate", p. 183.
47. Jack W. Wiley, Scott M. Brooks and Kyle M. Lundby, "Put Your Employees on the Other Side of the Microscope", *Human Resource Planning*, June 1, 2006, vol. 29, issue 2, pp. 15–21.
48. www.baldrigeplus.com, *Customer Satisfaction and Market Share at IBM Rochester*, Macpherson Publishing, Alexandra, New Zealand, 1999.
49. Frank J. Smith, *Organizational Surveys: The Diagnosis and Betterment of Organizations Through Their Members*, Lawrence Erlbaum Associates, 2003.
50. Anna Nyberg, Lars Alfredsson, Tores Theorell, Hugo Westerlund, Jussi Vahtera and Mika Kivimäki, "Managerial Leadership and Ischaemic Heart Disease Among Employees: The Swedish Wolf Study", *Occup. Environ. Med*, published online: Nov 27, 2008; doi:10.1136/oem.2008.039362
51. M. Kivimäki, M. Virtanen, M. Elovainio et al., "Work Stress in the Etiology of Coronary Heart Disease: A Meta-Analysis", *Scand J. Work Environ Health*, 2006, 32, pp. 431–2.
52. S. Setterlind and G. Larsson, "The Stress Profile: A Psychosocial Approach to Measuring Stress", *Stress Med*, 1995; 11, pp. 85–92.
53. Nyberg, Alfredsson, Theorell, Westerlund, Vahtera and Kivimäki, "Managerial Leadership and Ischaemic Heart Disease Among Employees", p. 5.
54. M. Kivimäki, J. E. Ferrie, E. Brunner et al., "Justice at Work and Reduced Risk of Coronary Heart Disease Among Employees: The Whitehall II Study", *Arch Intern Med*, 2005; 165, pp. 2245–51.
55. Ibid., p. 2246.
56. J. Siegrist, "Adverse Health Effects of High-Effort/Low-Reward Conditions", *J Occup Health Psychol*, 1996, Jan, 1 (1), pp. 27–41.

57. N. Wager, G. Fieldman and T. Hussey, "The Effect on Ambulatory Blood Pressure of Working Under Favourably and Unfavourably Perceived Supervisors", *Occup Environ Med*, 2003, 60, pp. 468–74, doi: 10.1136/oem. 60.7.468
58. M. G. Marmot, M. J. Shipley and G. Rose, "Inequalities in Death: Specific Explanations of a General Pattern", *Lancet*, 1984, 1, pp. 1003–7.
59. I. Kawachi, "Injustice at Work and Health: Causation or Correlation?" *Occup Environ Med*, 2006, 63, pp. 578–9.
60. Jane E. Ferrie, Jenny A. Head, Martin J. Shipley, Jussi Vahtera, Michael G. Marmot and Mika Kivimäki, "Injustice at Work and Health: Causation or Correlation", *Occupational and Environmental Medicine*, 2007, 64, p. 428. Copyright © 2007 by the BMJ Publishing Group Ltd.
61. H. Kuper and M. G. Marmot, "Job Strain, Job Demands, Decision Latitude, and Risk of Coronary Heart Disease Within the Whitehall II Study", *J Epidemiol Community Health*, 2003, 57, pp. 147–53.
62. H. Kuper, A. Singh-Manoux, J. Siegrist and M. Marmot, "When Reciprocity Fails: Effort Reward Within the Whitehall II Study", *Occup Environ Med*, 2002, 59, pp. 777–84.
63. M. Kivimäki, J. E. Ferrie, E. Brunner et al, "Justice at Work and Reduced Risk of Coronary Heart Disease Among Employees: The Whitehall II Study", *Arch Intern Med*, 2005, 165, p. 2247.
64. Wager, Fieldman and Hussey, "The Effect on Ambulatory Blood Pressure of Working Under Favourably and Unfavourably Perceived Supervisors".
65. M. Elovainio, M. Kivimäki and J. Vahtera, "Organizational Justice: Evidence of a New Psychosocial Predictor of Health", *Am J Public Health*, 2002, 92, pp. 105–08.
66. S. Cartwright and C. L. Cooper, *Oxford Handbook of Organizational Well-being*, Oxford: Oxford University Press, 2009.
67. M. Kivimäki, J. E. Ferrie, J. Head, M. J. Shipley, J. Vahtera and M. G. Marmot, "Organizational Justice and Change in Justice as Predictors of Employee Health: The Whitehall II Study", *J Epidemiol Community Health*, 2004, 58, pp. 931–7.

CREATING/MAINTAINING THE HIGH MORALE ORGANIZATION: DO WE CREATE HIGH MORALE – OR STEP OUT OF THE WAY?

1. http://www.accenture.com/Global/Research_and_Insights/By_Subject/ Talent_and_Organization/Human_Resources_Mgmt/HighPerformaceStud y2006.htm
2. Edward E. Lawler III, "The HR Department: Give it More Respect", *Wall Street Journal/MIT Sloan Management Review*, 3/10/2008 http:// sloanreview.mit.edu/business-insight/articles/2008/1/5016/the-hr-department-give-it-more-respect/; accessed on June 23, 2009.
3. C. L. Cooper and D. Bowles, *The Psychological Cost of Small Group Training*, UK Government Publication, 1976.

4. Robert A. G. Monks and Nell Minow, *Corporate Governance*, 3rd edition illustrated, Wiley-Blackwell, 2004, p. 350.
5. http://business.timesonline.co.uk/tol/business/industry_sectors/banking_and_finance/article4795072.ece
6. http://money.cnn.com/2009/02/11/news/companies/merrill_bonuses/index.htm
7. http://www.politico.com/news/stories/0309/20625.html
8. http://media.www.chibus.com/media/storage/paper408/news/2009/01/29/GsbNews/Wagoner-3627524.shtml
9. http://www.nbcbayarea.com/news/business/NATLWagoner-Will-Walk-With-23-Million.html

CURRENT TRENDS, ISSUES AND MYTHS IN EMPLOYEE MORALE

1. http://management.silicon.com/careers/0,39024671,39244967,00.htm
2. "Walking the Talk – Employer Ethics Statements Can Lower Morale", *HR Magazine*, October 2000, Copyright 2000 Society for Human Resource Management.
3. Ravi S. Gajendran and David A. Harrison (Pennsylvania State University), "The Good, the Bad, and the Unknown about Telecommuting: Meta-Analysis of Psychological Mediators and Individual Consequences", *Journal of Applied Psychology*, 2007, vol. 92, no. 6, pp. 1524–41. Copyright 2007 by the American Psychological Association.
4. http://www.apa.org/releases/telecommuting.html
5. Ron Alsop, *The Trophy Kids Grow Up: How the Millennial Generation is Shaking Up the Workplace*. Jossey-Bass. October 13, 2008.
6. http://www.telegraph.co.uk/news/uknews/1432411/Grade-creep-leads-86pc-of-students-to-expect-a-top-degree.html; accessed on June 23, 2009.
7. Ron Alsop, "The Trophy Kids Go to Work", *The Wall Street Journal*, http://sec.online.wsj.com/article/SB122455219391652725.html; accessed on October 21, 2008.
8. Carol Elam and Nicole Borges E., "Millennial in Medicine: A New Generation Comes to Medical School", 2008. http://www.med.wright.edu/aa/facdev/Events/2008info/millennials.ppt; accessed on June 23, 2009.
9. "In Taiwan, Unpaid Leave Instead of Layoffs Carries its Own Cost", *Los Angeles Times*, March 9, 2009.
10. Darrell Rigby, "Debunking Layoff Myths", available online at http://www.bain.com/bainweb/PDFs/cms/Public/BB_Debunking_layoff_myths.pdf
11. 1998 report from the Beth Israel Deaconess Medical Center in Boston, MA USA.
12. Sarah Moore, Leon Grunberg, Richard Anderson-Connolly and Edward S. Greenberg, "Physical and Mental Health Effects of Surviving Layoffs: A Longitudinal Examination", Institute Of Behavioral Science, Research

Program on Political and Economic Change, University of Colorado at Boulder; Working Paper PEC2003-0003, November 2003.
13. BWSmallBiz – Management, August 22, 2008, http://www.businessweek.com/magazine/content/08_68/s0808062563545.htm.
14. http://stevencerri.com/index.php/site/comments/71_9_8_08/.

EMPLOYEE MORALE AS A RESPONSE TO CHALLENGING TIMES

1. http://www.pinyin.info/chinese/crisis.html; accessed on June 23, 2009
2. http://www.independent.co.uk/opinion/commentators/douglas-mcwilliams-northern-rock-was-a-preventable-crisis-402706.html
3. *Los Angeles Times*, "Cheese Tells Tale of Europe's Meltdown", March 29, 2009, www.latimes.com
4. http://www.robertsoncooper.com/pages/todays-challenges/Business-Case-Wellbeing.aspx

INDEX